Inclusion:
what deaf pupils think

University of
Hertfordshire

RNID ● ❱❱❱

for deaf and hard of hearing people

Contents

Acknowledgements

The research team would like to thank the following institutions and people for their contributions to this project:

- the Department for Education and Skills for funding the project
- RNID – particularly Elizabeth Andrews, Stevie Mayhook, Jane Frew and Ruth Geall for their help, support and guidance
- Mary Read, Roman Pawluk, Chris Carter and Val Faulkner from the University of Hertfordshire
- Darren Saunders, for acting as Deaf consultant to the project
- and Marc Abbot for illustrations for some of the interview activities.

We would particularly like to thank the schools and services for all the time and effort involved in setting up the interview process and for welcoming us into their schools. Finally, we would like to thank all the pupils for their enthusiastic participation without which the project could not have been undertaken.

Foreword

This research is different, because it puts the views of young people centre stage.

Many policies have paid lip service to meeting the needs of children and young people with special educational needs in mainstream schools, but less has been done to find out what they themselves feel they need, as the recipients of policy and service initiatives.

The research project asked Key Stage 3 deaf pupils what they thought made a successful school and allowed pupils to flourish and what it was that they thought might be missing. It is unlikely that we will ever be able to make a success of inclusion if we do not find out from pupils themselves what makes a difference and if we do not listen to what they tell us.

Not only is this right in principle, but it also comes at a crucial time in the development of legislation and educational services for disabled children. The implementation of SENDA has given new impetus to the drive to ensure that deaf and hard of hearing children have the same access to educational opportunity as everyone else. The clearly stated principles within the legislation – of equal treatment and access to support – now have to backed up by real changes within the school system that will ensure principles are carried through into practice.

The research demonstrates that a focus on formal rights, though important, is not enough on its own. It points to areas where children need more support and change in practice and tells us that:

- Noise is an important factor determining whether deaf pupils in mainstream settings are able to learn or not. Schools have a responsibility to audit noise levels, identify areas in which listening conditions are particularly poor and to do something about it.

- Mainstream teachers must know how to modify their standard classroom delivery to meet the special educational needs of deaf pupils and use appropriate strategies consistently. It is the responsibility of schools to provide an ongoing programme of professional development in this area, to monitor the classroom delivery of teachers with deaf pupils in their class, and to make sure that supply teachers know what to do.

- While they value their friendships with hearing children, deaf pupils also want and need to meet other deaf pupils.

- Support from adults is critical, but counter-productive where it becomes interference and impedes group discussion and social inclusion.

It is instructive that while policy initiatives are typically focused on increasing access to the curriculum, the children told us that social exclusion and friendship with their hearing peers was what was really important to them. Social inclusion is a crucial, but often neglected element determining whether or not children benefit from their time in education.

Policy-makers need to take note of the comments made by this sample of pupils and respond, if the aspirations we all have for inclusion within the classroom are to become a reality. Actions speak louder than words.

The education system has a unique opportunity over the next few years to put into place the changes needed to make schools accessible to pupils with special educational needs and disabilities. There is established good practice to build on, and what pupils say should be central to the process of development from this point onwards. It is for us all to listen to the views reported here and to act on them.

Brian Lamb
Director of Communications
RNID

Preface

Research team biographies

The research team comprised two members of teaching staff and a research fellow from the University of Hertfordshire, supported by a Deaf consultant.

Darren Saunders acted as the Deaf consultant. He is a lecturer at the University of Reading and a British Sign Language (BSL) user. He has experience of leading drama workshops and of facilitating literacy projects for deaf children.

The research fellow was **Alessandra Iantaffi** who is a teacher and a linguist with extensive research experience, including research involving recording the experiences of individuals and groups. She achieved her PhD in 1999, winning the BERA dissertation award for that year. She gained her CACDP Stage 3 qualification in BSL in 1995 and has worked with Friends for Young Deaf People and on Deaf@x projects. She has also worked as an interpreter in higher education. She was a researcher on *Deafness, Design and Communication in the Built Environment* (Crystal Project), investigating the effects of light and colour in buildings on deaf people's ease of communication.

The project investigators were from the departments of Linguistics and Education at the University. **Indra Sinka** is a teacher and a linguist and has research experience in the field of child language and bilingualism. She gained her PhD in 1999 in child language acquisition. She was project manager for the restandardisation of the Reynell Language Development Scale 3 and was an investigator on the Crystal Project. She was a literacy support tutor for deaf students at the University of Reading for four years, taught linguistics at the University of Hertfordshire, and has recently moved as Staff Tutor to the Faculty of Education and Language Studies at the Open University.

Joy Jarvis has been a teacher of the deaf for over 20 years and has worked in a range of contexts with deaf children and young people. She is currently leading the University of Hertfordshire's course for training teachers of the deaf. She has close links with schools and services for deaf children and is involved in a range of professional development activities, including work with the British Association of Teachers of the Deaf.

Time frame

The research project ran from November 2001 to July 2002 and was split into 10 phases, some running concurrently. The first three phases (from November 2001 to January 2002) saw the design of the one-to-one interviews, an in-depth literature review, school contacts established, and a pilot study and its analysis. Phases 4 and 5 (January to March 2002) focused on the main data collection and analysis for the one-to-one interviews.

Phases 6 and 7 (January to April 2002) saw the design and recording of the focus group interviews. Phases 8, 9 and 10 (May to July 2002) comprised of final analyses and the drafting of this report.

The ongoing project was discussed with a number of teachers of the deaf during in-service training sessions, including the SENJIT conference for teachers of the deaf in London in June 2002. The methodology was discussed at academic conferences at the universities of Warwick and Florence in the Spring of 2002 and also at the British Education Research Association conference.

Funding

This research project was funded by a grant from the Department for Education and Skills (DfES).

Terminology

For the purposes of simplicity the term 'deaf' is used throughout this report to describe any child with an educationally significant hearing loss (ie a hearing loss >40dB in the better ear). Mild, moderate, severe and profound levels of deafness are defined according to the normal professional convention:

British Society of Audiology (BSA) definitions of level of hearing loss:
Mild   average hearing loss in better ear of 20-40dBHL
Moderate   average hearing loss in better ear of 41-70dBHL
Severe   average hearing loss in better ear of 71-95dBHL
Profound   average hearing loss in better ear of 95+dBHL

'Pupil' is used to refer to children who are of statutory school age.

Abbreviations and terms unfamiliar to readers may be found in the Glossary at the end of this publication.

Chapter 1

Executive summary

Executive summary

The purpose of the research project was to document deaf and hearing pupils' experiences of the inclusion of deaf children in mainstream classrooms. At a time when, increasingly, deaf children are being included in mainstream schools it was identified as essential to obtain the pupil perspective on this process. Specific aims were to identify barriers to inclusion, factors facilitating inclusion and to consider both academic and social aspects of inclusion.

The participants

Data were gathered from 83 Key Stage 3 pupils from Years 7, 8 and 9 attending 25 schools in 16 areas across England. Pupils (of whom, 61 were deaf) were chosen to represent a range of communication modes and differing levels of deafness and a small number of hearing pupils were also included in the project. Pupils either attended a mainstream school with some form of unit provision, or were individually included in their local mainstream school.

Methodology

Two methods of data collection were employed during the project: one-to-one interviews and focus group discussions. Only deaf pupils were interviewed on a one-to-one-basis, while both deaf and hearing pupils were involved in focus groups. A range of activities was undertaken in both contexts to identify pupils' perspectives on their experiences in mainstream schools.

Key findings

Identity: Pupils' views on deafness (Chapter 4)

- Pupils' descriptions of themselves as hearing, deaf or one of a range of descriptions between did not always reflect their actual degree of hearing loss.

- There were both perceived advantages and disadvantages in disclosing your deafness to hearing pupils. Advantages included the possibility of better communication, while disadvantages included other people treating you differently from hearing people, asking intrusive questions or teasing you.

- Deaf pupils liked having other deaf pupils in the school as they found communication with them easier and were with others who understood their situation. They generally liked being with hearing pupils too as it helped the two groups get on together.

School ethos (Chapter 5)

- The majority of pupils interviewed described their school in positive terms.

- Valuing diversity seemed to be an important aspect of school ethos.

- Pupils had both positive and negative experiences of communicating with teachers and hearing pupils.

- The level of deaf awareness of both staff and pupils varied greatly, both within and between schools.

- Some, but by no means all, hearing pupils receive deaf awareness training as part of their school activities.

- Deaf pupils tend to accept that deaf awareness activities need to take place but would prefer these not to be related to particular deaf pupils.

- Few deaf pupils were aware of what an equal opportunities policy was or if their school had one.

- Most pupils saw withdrawal from mainstream classes for additional work in a unit context as a bridge towards full-time inclusion.

- Most of the deaf pupils did not perceive themselves as being involved in the planning process which determined how their needs should be met.

Staff roles (Chapter 6)

- Pupils' perceived a range of staff as being responsible for their learning.

- Pupils saw mainstream teachers as having positive roles in terms of explaining, helping, understanding, being approachable and dealing with other pupils if they caused problems. They had negative roles in relation to giving homework and monitoring work and behaviour closely.

- The role of peripatetic teachers of the deaf was seen to include: providing support in some lessons, assessing support needs, checking equipment and explaining about deafness.

- The role of unit teachers of the deaf was seen to be: to help with homework, tests, revision and particular subjects, to assess support needs, to coordinate support staff and to give emotional support to deaf pupils.

- The role of teaching assistants (TAs) was seen to include helping with communication and with understanding mainstream teachers. A function was to encourage pupils to work and to be available when needed. Negative aspects of the role included a perceived tendency to over-explain things and to be always there, even when not needed.

- The role of communication support workers (CSWs) was seen to include notetaking, signing and helping pupils to understand in the classroom, to provide support in tests and exams and to be easy to communicate with. Negative aspects of the role seemed to be to help too much and to be intrusive.

Academic inclusion (Chapter 7)

- Pupils saw factors which facilitated academic inclusion as: clear communication, teachers being understanding, good deaf awareness among staff, appropriate use of audiological equipment, pupils being open about deafness and asking for help, friends supporting each other and a good school environment.

- Pupils saw factors which are barriers to academic inclusion as: poor communication, lack of deaf awareness, poor use of audiological equipment by teachers, lack of or insufficient support, noise, teachers not acknowledging deaf pupils' difficulties and deaf pupils being socially excluded by peers.

- Homework was not seen as a particular problem except that it was not always explained clearly.

- Exams were not seen as a particular problem except when tape recordings were used or because support staff could not give pupils the support they were used to receiving in the classroom.

- Most pupils used the full range of school facilities and some also used equipment, such as computers, available in some units.

- The majority of pupils, regardless of their level of hearing loss, commented about noise interfering in their school lives. This included noise from other pupils, from teachers shouting or specific rooms that had poor acoustics.

- All the deaf pupils interviewed agreed that equipment, such as radio aids, made their hearing loss visible to others which could be embarrassing.

- Pupils saw mainstream teachers' behaviour in relation to the use of audiological equipment as erratic. Not all teachers seem to like to use, or know how to use, radio aids appropriately.

- The majority of deaf pupils received some in-class support. This did not usually cover all lessons and some pupils found that lack of support in lessons made them hard to follow.

- Pupils commented on a wide range of awareness and expertise in relation to mainstream teachers' communication skills. Communication with teachers of the deaf was usually seen as easier.

- The reasons for liking or disliking a particular curriculum subject were usually linked to the teacher's way of teaching. Practical and interactive strategies were preferred by all the pupils interviewed. Subjects where there was a significant amount of teacher talk or discussion, or where there was a lot of noise, were disliked.

- Teaching strategies that were seen as helpful included: practical or interactive approaches, clear explanations and fun activities. Unhelpful strategies were: talking too much, not explaining things properly and being boring.

- The pupils interviewed saw working together with other pupils as more fun than working alone. It was also seen as more effective as pupils could help each other. They commented that teachers sometimes moved them so that they were not sitting with their friends; however, pupils saw sitting near their friends as important in a group work context where communication can be difficult.

- Hearing pupils thought that deaf pupils generally managed well in a classroom context.

- Hearing pupils commented that mainstream teachers varied in their deaf awareness and their ability to communicate with deaf pupils. They commented that some teachers found equipment, such as radio aids, difficult to use. They felt that sometimes teachers gave too much help to deaf pupils. They identified that noise can be an issue in lessons.

Social inclusion (Chapter 8)

- All the deaf pupils talked about friendship extensively and saw it as a key aspect of school life. Deaf pupils wanted to be treated the same as anyone else, yet they appreciated their friends understanding that they were deaf as well.

- Communication between deaf and hearing pupils was seen as an issue, which could be helped by time and experience to a certain extent. Because of these difficulties some deaf pupils preferred to communicate with other deaf pupils rather than with hearing pupils.

- Most deaf pupils took part in after-school social activities, either connected with the school or outside.

- Some deaf pupils saw the unit in their school as a safe place, where they could communicate easily and relax. Some pupils were concerned that attending the unit made them more visible and could isolate them from hearing pupils.

- Some pupils interviewed had been teased or bullied but this was not always seen as being related to their deafness. Pupils thought that usually school staff intervened appropriately or pupils dealt with it themselves.

- Hearing pupils felt that communication could be a barrier to social inclusion and they appreciated that not everyone in the school community understood deafness to the extent that they did. There were a number of things they would have liked to ask deaf pupils about deafness but felt that it was a sensitive subject.

Summary: findings and recommendations (Chapter 9)

In relation to deaf peers and adults,
schools need to:

- consider the role of deaf peers in the education of deaf pupils
- consider the role of deaf adults in the education of deaf pupils

In relation to teaching roles,
teachers of the deaf need to:

- continue to support deaf pupils in relation to their academic, personal and social needs
- consult with pupils about their support

In relation to mainstream teaching,
teachers need to:

- be aware of, and use, appropriate strategies during lessons without drawing attention to individuals

schools need to:

- provide ongoing professional development for teachers
- monitor the use of appropriate classroom strategies
- provide a system for giving relevant information to supply teachers

In relation to equipment and noise,
teachers of the deaf need to:

- ensure that equipment is suitable for the context and is appropriately adjusted

mainstream teachers need to:

- consider the effect of noise on hearing aid users
- identify ways of managing audiological equipment unobtrusively

schools need to:

- identify poor acoustic environments and seek to improve these

In relation to adult support,
support staff need to:

- continue to give effective, targeted support to individuals
- not over-support
- provide support for the lesson and the teacher as well as the pupil

schools and teachers of the deaf need to:

- provide high quality training for all those providing support
- monitor support work
- provide timetabled sessions for support planning

In relation to peer support,
schools and teachers of the deaf need to:

- provide deaf awareness sessions for hearing pupils
- discuss the deaf awareness sessions with deaf pupils
- provide sessions for deaf pupils on strategies to use with hearing peers
- raise the profile of deafness within the school environment, the curriculum and teaching approaches

In relation to monitoring the success of inclusion,
schools need to:

- identify ways of obtaining pupils' perceptions on their provision

Chapter 2

Setting the scene

Setting the scene

The inclusion of deaf children in mainstream contexts is not a new phenomenon. By the 1970s units on the site of mainstream schools were well established for children with a hearing loss. Since then, however, there has been a gradual movement towards children spending more time in mainstream classes, and being placed in their local school. Inclusion has a high priority in the UK's social and educational agenda and is part of the attempt to move towards a more inclusive and equitable society. In turn this relates to an international inclusive movement aiming to deliver equal opportunities for all.

Definitions of inclusion vary and do not necessarily involve the placement of all children in mainstream settings. Nevertheless the Special Educational Needs Code of Practice (2001) emphasises: "the special educational needs of children will normally be met in mainstream schools or settings". There are perceived advantages for children with special educational needs being educated with their peers in mainstream contexts, rather than in special schools, which including wider social opportunities and access to a mainstream curriculum with associated expectations of achievement. Perceived advantages for mainstream children include the raising of awareness of a range of needs, an improved acceptance of difference and the development of skills to interact with a variety of people.

A number of issues regarding mainstream placements have been raised in relation to deaf pupils. There is little robust research evidence to demonstrate whether inclusion does or does not confer the academic benefits expected for this population (cf the bibliography for literature sources on this topic). Social inclusion may be adversely affected by communication difficulties. A deaf peer group will only be available if deaf children are placed together in a resourced school (ie a mainstream school with a resourced base for deaf pupils, or unit). Deaf adults to provide role models and communication support for deaf pupils included in mainstream schools on an individual basis are not commonly available.

Perspectives

RNID's *A Review of Good Practice in Deaf Education* (Powers et al 1999) and its supplement (Gregory et al 2001) asked what young deaf adults, parents, educators and organisations working with deaf people considered to be good practice in the education of deaf children. The development of pupils' self-esteem, access to a full curriculum and the development of communication skills were seen as essential. Some people saw mainstream placement delivering this provision: positive aspects were seen to be opportunities for increased achievement and exposure to spoken and written English. Others saw communication difficulties with teachers and hearing peers, low expectations of deaf pupils on the part of some teachers, limited understanding of the needs of deaf children and lack of deaf awareness as barriers to effective inclusion.

What do pupils themselves think about inclusion? The UN Convention on the Rights of the Child (1989) raised the profile of children's rights worldwide and underlined the importance of listening to children's views. In the UK, the Children Act (1989) and the Code of Practice on Special Educational Needs (2001) stress the right of the child to be consulted about provision. Children's experience of an educational placement may be vastly different from that assumed by the adults involved.

There have been a number of projects undertaken to identify pupils' perceptions of inclusion. In 1990 the UK National Deaf Children's Society published the results of a survey in which 129 secondary-aged pupils in resourced units in mainstream schools responded in writing to questions about their experiences. A range of views was expressed, including both positive and negative aspects of education in a mainstream context. In relation to academic aspects of education some pupils reported issues with academic inclusion due to difficulties understanding communication in a classroom context. One pupil commented: "I reckon that half of school for me is actually figuring out and jigsawing together what is said". In relation to social aspects, some children reported difficulties communicating with hearing peers and with being bullied. Gregory et al (1995) interviewed 71 young deaf adults about their experiences of growing up, including their opinions and experiences of education. Approximately a quarter favoured some form of mainstream provision for deaf pupils but very few thought that the placement of one deaf child in a mainstream school was appropriate: "...there shouldn't be one deaf pupil on their own in a class of hearing pupils but four or five in each class. I know the frustration of being on my own – my tension and frustration" (Phillip, 19 years, page 64).

Now is a good time for a new study to be undertaken to identify deaf pupils' perceptions of inclusion; being part of a mainstream class, for at least some of their time in school, is an increasingly common part of deaf children's experience. The move from the concept of 'integration' to 'inclusion' implies that schools should be identifying ways in which they can adapt their provision to meet the needs of a range of pupils with special educational needs (SEN). This is emphasised by the implementation of the Special Educational Needs and Disability Act (SENDA 2001) which is imposing new responsibilities on mainstream schools in relation to disabled children from September 2002. There is greater awareness of deaf people in society, partly due to the role of pressure groups and to more evidence of the use of sign language in the media. Increasing inclusion of children with special needs in general has led to improved policies and practices for SEN in schools and, in most places, to increased staff resources to support this process. In relation to deaf children, earlier diagnosis implies greater access to communication at an earlier age and therefore improved access to language and literacy when they start school. Technology has improved, leading to more deaf children having greater access to spoken language, while approaches to the development and use of British Sign Language (BSL) are also better understood.

Self-advocacy is playing an increasingly important role in education today and the voice of the pupil is being heard in a range of contexts. A recent study by the National Deaf Children's Society (Scotland) (2001a) involved interviews with 42 deaf young people between the ages of 11 and 21. Issues identified mirrored many of those found in earlier studies. Some pupils reported positive experiences of inclusion with hearing friends and an increased confidence in their ability to function in a hearing world. Others, however, had difficulties accessing the curriculum because of inappropriate teacher strategies and reported some social isolation, instances of bullying and some difficulties with identity.

To what extent has the situation changed since earlier studies? In 1990 one deaf pupil wrote about the placement of deaf children in mainstream schools: "Integration would make life easier for many people, combining their ideas and hopes. But parents and teachers must know how the deaf children feel." (NCDS 1990, page 14). This project is an attempt to find out how a representative sample of deaf pupils felt about their experiences of inclusion in 2002.

Chapter 3

Research design and implementation

Research design and implementation

Aims of the project

> The aims of the project were:
>
> - to document and disseminate deaf pupils' experiences of inclusion
>
> - to identify barriers and factors facilitating the effective inclusion of deaf pupils into mainstream schools

The main purpose of the research was to record deaf pupils' personal experiences of attending mainstream schools. A secondary aim was to record the perspectives of hearing pupils who had deaf children in their classes. In this way a picture could be built of how both groups of children perceived the same context. Activities were designed so that pupils could identify issues that were important to them. Analysis of pupils' responses to the activities would lead to the identification of themes within the group's experiences, to an understanding of what pupils saw as positive and negative within their contexts, and what they saw as supporting or limiting their inclusion.

The participants

Participants' profile

> Overall:
>
> - 83 Key Stage 3 pupils from Years 7, 8 and 9 were interviewed during the project
>
> - data was gathered from 25 different schools in 16 areas across England
>
> - pupils were chosen to represent a range of communication modes and different levels of deafness

In total, 83 Key Stage 3 pupils were interviewed for the project. Key Stage 3 was chosen as the focus, as it was felt that pupils at this stage would have recent experience of at least two educational settings (eg primary and secondary) and would be mature enough to articulate their thoughts and feelings. The participants were categorised according to year group, gender, level of deafness and the communication mode preferred by the participants for the interview. For purposes of clarity, the terms 'cochlear/cochlear implant' are used throughout this report to represent those pupils with a profound level of deafness who have been fitted with a cochlear implant device. The terms 'oral' and 'signing' are used to identify the pupils' preferred modes of communication during the interviews; other modes of communication may well be employed by pupils either during the school day or at home. The term 'signing' is used to indicate where pupils have chosen to make use of BSL, Total Communication (TC) or Sign Supported English (SSE). The overall figures are represented below, in Table 1:

Table 1 – participants' profile

Year group			Gender		Level of hearing/deafness					Communication mode	
7	8	9	M	F	Hearing	Moderate	Severe	Profound	Cochlear Implant	Signing	Oral
29	32	22	39	44	22	19	17	21	4	27	34

Figure 1 below shows the distribution of the total number of deaf pupils according to both level of deafness and communication mode:

Figure 1 Communication mode and level of deafness

Oral – front row
Signing – back row

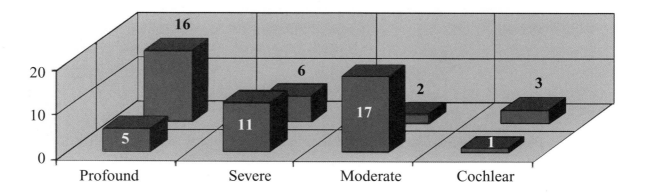

28% of the participants came from a variety of ethnic minority groups, including Asian, Black Caribbean, Arabic and non-British European.

The data were collected through one-to-one interviews (deaf pupils only) and focus group discussions (deaf and hearing pupils). The figures and graphs below show the profile of the pupils across the two groups:

One-to-one interviews
39 deaf pupils were interviewed during this phase of the project – 19 male, 20 female. Their levels of deafness and choice of communication mode are presented here:

Figure 2 Level of deafness

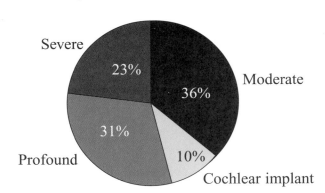

Figure 3 Communication mode

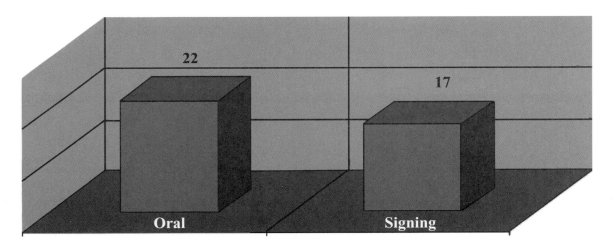

Focus groups

44 pupils, of whom 20 were male and 24 female, were interviewed in group situations. In total there were 22 deaf and 22 hearing pupils and each focus group had a minimum of three and a maximum of six participants. Altogether there were 10 focus groups in five schools, with each school providing one deaf and one hearing group, which made for some interesting comparisons within schools. The level of hearing/deafness and the deaf pupils' choice of communication mode during the focus group interviews is given below:

Figure 4 Level of hearing/deafness

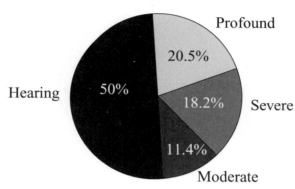

Figure 5 Communication mode

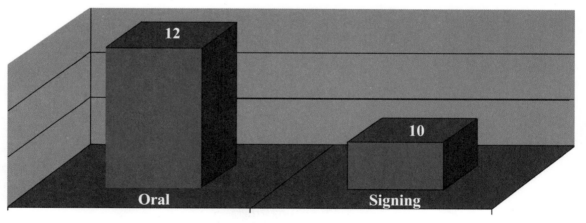

Schools' profile

In November 2001, 64 schools and services were contacted with details of the proposed project and the response from them was overwhelmingly positive. The final data sample of schools and pupils was then chosen to ensure as reasonable as possible a spread of type of school provision, year group, gender, mode of communication and range of hearing loss.

Figure 6 below shows the distribution of the schools according to type of provision – mainstream (without dedicated unit), mainstream with hearing impaired unit (HIU) and mainstream with special educational needs (SEN) base (it is recognised by the research team that schools may use a variety of terms to describe their provision):

Figure 6 Provision within schools

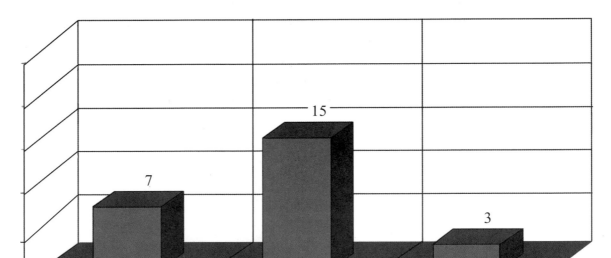

Type of provision

The project also aimed to achieve as wide a geographical spread as possible; the distribution of schools in the 16 areas across England is represented in Figure 7.

Figure 7 Distribution of schools

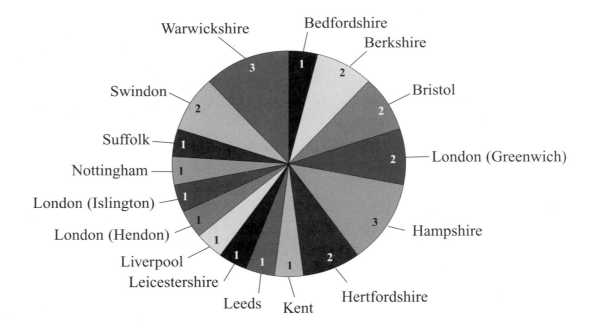

Methodology

Two methods of data collection were employed during the project:

- one-to-one interviews
- focus group discussions

Only deaf pupils were interviewed on a one-to-one basis.
Both deaf and hearing pupils were involved in the focus groups.
Both deaf and hearing researchers were involved in the data collection.
All activities were piloted.
All interviews and discussions were audio- and video-recorded.

Pilot study

Following the design of the one-to-one interviews, a pilot study was carried out on six pupils in three geographical areas. Of these six pupils, five chose to use oral communication during the interviews and one opted to sign. The level of hearing loss was split equally between severe and moderate. All the pilot pupils attended schools with either unit provision or SEN bases.

The methodology employed during the pilot study proved appropriate for the project design and as no amendments were made to the strategies applied, the six pupils involved in the pilot were included in the main sample reported on here.

One-to-one interviews

All one-to-one interviews were carried out using the communication mode chosen by the pupil for the interview. Consent was obtained from the schools and parents of the pupils involved in the research and each pupil was advised that they could opt out of the interview at any point should they wish to do so. In order to ensure comparability and reliability across the interviews, the same pattern and variety of questions and activities was presented to all pupils. Pupils presented their responses through sign, speech or the written form; during the writing tasks, pupils could choose to either write down thoughts and ideas themselves or, if preferred, have these written down for them by the interviewer.

Each one-to-one interview started with questions to put pupils at their ease. These included general questions concerning their present and previous schools and how the pupils described themselves in relation to their hearing loss; the term used by a pupil (eg "I'm deaf/hearing/hearing impaired") was then employed by the interviewer when necessary during the interview.

Questions and activities

Metaphor

Pupils were asked: "Imagine that you had to move home and go to a different school, a long way away from here; what is the one thing that you would take with you to remind you of school?" The pupils were then asked to give reasons for their choices.

General factors facilitating or creating barriers to inclusion in a pupil's school

Pupils were asked to list both the positive and negative aspects of life at school ("what things make your life at school better or worse?"); these were presented on a 'mind map' containing the following image:

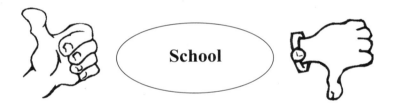

Academic inclusion

The pupils were asked to comment about various issues related to academic inclusion (eg "Can you tell me about your favourite subject? Why do you like it? How is it taught?") and responses were listed by the interviewer on a repertory grid. (Repertory grids are additional effective research tools and here were used to elicit pupils' comments on their mainstream environment. Trends in the pupils' responses could then be identified more easily.) The following were the issues addressed directly by the interviewer:

- favourite subject

- least favourite subject

- library, IT and other facilities used in school

- homework

- tests

- other adults (excluding mainstream teacher) supporting a pupil's learning [this included adults both at school and at home]

Pupils were also asked to "think about the helpful and unhelpful things that teachers do in the classroom". Their views were presented on paper under the following illustrated heading:

Things that teachers do

Social inclusion
During the interview pupils were asked about their participation in social activities both in and outside school and about their relationships with their deaf and hearing peers.

Three puppets (large rag dolls) were used to develop the following role-play situations:

1) I would like to introduce you to my friends, here [interviewer indicates the puppets];
I would like you to imagine that they are your age, that this boy has a hearing loss like you and that these two [one girl, one boy] are hearing. This deaf [or another term used by the pupil] boy is going to come to your school next year; what advice would you give him?

2) These hearing children [interviewer indicates the other two puppets] are going to be in the same class as the deaf [or another term used by the pupil] boy; what could you tell them that would help them be friends with the deaf [or another term used by the pupil] boy? Is there any particular advice you would give?

School policies and procedures
Pupils were asked whether they knew what an equal opportunities policy was and also whether their school had such a policy and where it was kept.

Focus groups

Analysis of the one-to-one interviews led to confirmation and/or identification of themes for discussion during the focus group meetings. Each school participating in the focus group discussions provided both deaf and hearing groups of pupils; as a result of this, interesting similarities and contrasts were observed in the comments from groups within the same school.

Topics for discussion in the focus groups included:

- general comments about the pupils' schools

- identity

- communication support

- equipment (eg radio aids)

- deaf and hearing friends

- mainstream teachers

- communication (with both adults and peers) in one-to-one situations

- communication (with both adults and peers) in group situations

- bullying

- advice to deaf/hearing pupils

- tests/exams

- the unit

- deaf awareness

Other activities

The three puppets were used with the focus groups in the same way as during the one-to-one interviews.

Pictures [simple line drawings] were used to encourage discussion of issues relating to communication in both one-to-one and group situations. The following questions were asked of the pupils:

a)   using a picture showing one-to-one communication:
     "What happens when you're with a deaf/hearing pupil on your own?"

b)   using a picture showing a group situation:
     "What happens when you're in a group with deaf/hearing pupils – in class?"
     "What happens when you're in a group with deaf/hearing pupils – during break time?"

The final activity for the focus groups was for each pupil to write individually on a 'speech bubble', giving advice or asking a question that they have always wished to ask of a deaf or hearing person: deaf pupils wrote to hearing pupils and hearing pupils wrote to deaf pupils. "Think of a deaf/hearing pupil in your class or school. What would you like to say to them/ask them?"

Analysis

Transcription and data analysis

All recordings were transcribed as soon as possible after data collection. All transcriptions of signed interviews were verified by a native BSL user; oral interviews were transcribed making use of both video and audio recordings. Pupil responses were collated after the interviews and important issues related to inclusion were then identified.

Software used to analyse the data included the programs SPSS, for statistical analysis and Atlas.ti 4.2; Atlas.ti 4.2 was used to aid analysis of the repertory grids and to highlight vocabulary used by the pupils to describe their experiences of inclusion. For example, when describing themselves, pupils used varied terminology (eg 'deaf', 'a little bit deaf', 'partially hearing', 'hearing') which can be easily represented in chart form, showing associations and links between the different terms used (cf the charts in figures 8, 9, 10, 11 and 14).

Conclusion

All the pupils involved in the research project responded openly and in-depth to the questions posed and activities presented to them. This generated a wealth of information about the issues identified as important to the children. This information has been grouped under various themes during analysis and is presented in Chapters 4, 5, 6, 7 and 8. Chapter 4 presents a summary of the views held by both deaf and hearing pupils about deafness, whilst Chapter 5 addresses the school environment and its ethos as seen by the pupils; Chapter 6 explores the roles staff play in school life. Finally, Chapters 7 and 8 illustrate in more detail the pupils' experiences of academic and social inclusion. In these chapters, the pupils' own words are used wherever possible, in order that the reader may listen to stories and experiences as described by the pupils themselves. The quotations are in random order, which reflects the spontaneity of the pupils' responses and are not classified to present a particular viewpoint.

Chapter 4

Identity:
pupils' views on deafness

Identity: pupils' views on deafness

Introduction

The development of personal identity is a complex, ongoing issue which is of particular significance to children of secondary school age. A number of factors are involved in developing a sense of individual identity and how one fits into society, including gender, ethnicity, social class, family, personality, relationship with peers and different adults. For deaf children, other factors to consider include: the presence of a hearing loss, the hearing status of other family members, communication within the family and attitudes to deafness (Sheridan 2002). In relation to school, factors which influence the developing deaf young person's sense of self may include the presence, or not, of other deaf pupils, the role of deaf adults within the school community, how deaf issues are addressed, school ethos (particularly in relation to difference), teachers' and hearing pupils' attitudes to deafness and communication between all parties (Stinson and Foster 2000).

All pupils were asked, at the beginning of the interview, how they would describe themselves in relation to their hearing loss, so that the interviewer could mirror the pupil's own labels, rather than impose a particular term. Sometimes this information emerged naturally at the beginning of the interview, before the question was asked.

It soon became clear that the terminology provided by the pupils to describe their hearing loss, such as, for example 'deaf' or 'hearing impaired', reflected how they saw themselves and others and was linked to their experiences of inclusion, communication with teachers and other pupils and friendship. Therefore, before looking at the data as they relate to the main project's aims, it is useful to present a summary of such views. Figure 8 illustrates how the threads emerging from the data relate to the topic of deafness and identity. The symbol == means 'is associated with', whilst [ ] means 'is part of'.

Figure 8 Data on deafness and identity

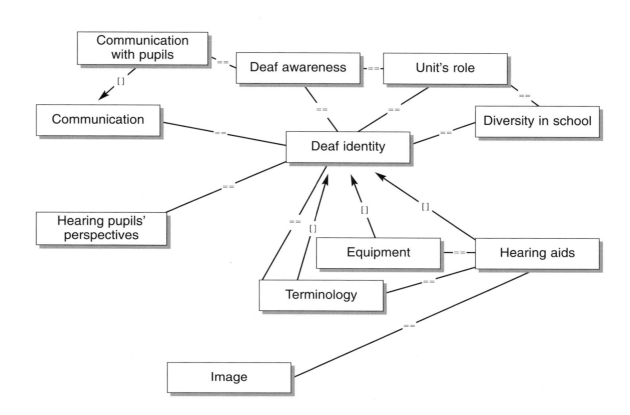

How would you describe yourself?

The pupils' terminology when describing themselves in relation to their hearing loss varied between two opposite poles, hearing and deaf, covering various degrees in between.

Their choice of words did not always reflect their actual degree of hearing loss. Some pupils with a moderate loss were happy to describe themselves as deaf, whilst others were happier referring to themselves as hearing or partially hearing. However, the pupils with severe and profound hearing losses were, generally, those who were most comfortable with the word 'deaf'. The majority of the pupils described themselves as partially hearing or partially deaf.

What the pupils who see themselves as hearing say

"Partially hearing, probably more hearing than not hearing." (Year 9 male pupil, moderate hearing loss, oral)

"Hearing" (Year 9 female pupil, profound hearing loss, cochlear implant, oral)

"I'd say I'm alright actually, normal hearing." (Year 9 female pupil, moderate hearing loss, oral)

What the pupils who see themselves as partially deaf say

"I'm not totally deaf, I would describe myself as a little bit deaf." (Year 7 male pupil, moderate hearing loss, oral)

"I would say I'm deaf but not, like, totally. Just try to be as normal as I can with it." (Year 8 male pupil, moderate hearing loss, oral)

"I'm not that deaf because I can hear properly now but sometimes I just can't hear properly." (Year 8 male pupil, moderate hearing loss, oral)

"I usually say I'm deaf or I can't hear very well. 'Cause I'm not like proper deaf but I am deaf in a way." (Year 7 male pupil, moderate hearing loss, oral)

"I'm just over a quarter deaf so I just normally say hard of hearing." (Year 8 female pupil, moderate hearing loss, oral)

What the pupils who see themselves as deaf say

"I just say I've got hearing aids because I'm deaf and when I take them out I can't hear anything." (Year 7 female pupil, profound hearing loss, oral)

"Deaf" (Year 8 female pupil, severe hearing loss, oral)

"I'm profoundly deaf and I lipread a little bit." (Year 9 female pupil, profound hearing loss, signing)

"I am deaf." (Year 9 male pupil, profound hearing loss, cochlear implant, signing)

"Sometimes I think I'm deaf." (Year 7 female pupil, moderate hearing loss, oral)

"I tend not to tell people I'm deaf unless they find out … and then they asked me, I'd go 'yeah, I am' but I wouldn't tell them." (Year 8 female pupil, moderate hearing loss, oral)

"I wouldn't unless they needed to know – if they spoke really quietly or didn't look at me and I needed to." (Year 8 female pupil, profound hearing loss, oral)

Interacting with hearing people

As illustrated by the last two quotes in the previous section, the pupils take into consideration their hearing loss when interacting with others, whether they choose to conceal it or to disclose it. In either case the pupils are aware that disclosing their deafness might affect people's reaction. This is an issue that will be explored in more depth when addressing the themes related to social inclusion.

What pupils say

The advantages of disclosing their hearing loss are:

- others are going to notice anyway
- they can explain what their communication needs are
- people speak more clearly
- it can make them feel special

"Don't pretend there's not a problem, there is. Well, it's not a problem but you have to explain to people, otherwise they don't understand and that causes a big problem." (Year 8 female pupil, moderate hearing loss, oral)

"I don't care what people think of my deafness. I wouldn't mind telling the truth. There is no point lying, they're going to find out the truth sooner or later." (Year 9 male pupil, profoundly deaf, oral)

"You just tell them what really is. You shouldn't lie, unless you don't feel fully confident in telling them really." (Year 8 male pupil, severe hearing loss, oral)

"I'm profoundly deaf and I either lipread or ask them to write down what they wanted to say." (Year 7 male pupil, profound hearing loss, signing)

"If they ask me if I was deaf, I would say yes. If they tried to speak to me I tend to mime to communicate with them." (Year 9 female pupil, profound hearing loss, signing)

"The person with hearing aids is still normal like you, they're no different. Try and speak clearly with them so they can hear you properly. Try and be patient if they ask you something and they just keep on asking you what the teacher said or something and they want you to repeat it." (Year 9 female pupil, moderate hearing loss, oral – advice given to the hearing puppets)

"It's easier, it makes hearing people speak clearer." (Year 8 male pupil, moderate hearing loss, signing)

"You sort of feel kind of special because you've got hearing aids and things so that was a good thing." (Year 8 female pupil, moderate hearing loss, oral)

"To make friends is quite easy because I got a friend. She befriended me because she wanted to know what it's like to be deaf and I told her all about it and she goes 'cool' and all that." (Year 7 female pupil, moderate hearing loss, oral)

The disadvantages of disclosing their hearing loss are:

- people ask questions
- they might be teased or bullied because of the hearing loss
- people over-articulate their speech
- others treat them strangely

"When I first went to my primary school, everyone was always staring at my ears because no one had seen hearing aids before and I'd say try to forget they're there and treat him as if he's hearing as well." (Year 8 female pupil, moderate hearing loss, oral – advice given to the hearing puppets)

"I wouldn't ask many, many questions about being deaf. I mean, like 'does it hurt' or something. Just be there, just talk directly to his face but just pretend that he's not deaf, just pretend that he's like you." (Year 8 female pupil, severe hearing loss, oral – advice given to the hearing puppets)

"When me and my friend were in Year 7, we had a lot of people asking us questions. We got a little bit fed up but we didn't mind answering but as it came the same question all the time, it annoyed us a little bit. But, like, in Year 8 they did ask many questions and now they treat us like normal, we're just like hearing people to them." (Year 9 male pupil, severe hearing loss, oral)

"They call me cabbage because I can't follow speech well." (Year 9 female pupil, profound hearing loss, signing)

"There's some quite friendly people around here but some of them, because we're deaf, sometimes they just ignore us and they don't respect us all the time." (Year 8 male pupil, moderate hearing loss, oral)

"I prefer sometimes people not to know 'cause some people tend to act strangely. ... They kind of talk over-dramatically and say H-E-L-L-O... And it's easier if they just talked normally. I just say, 'please, don't do that'. I prefer it if you talk normally. I'm not stupid." (Year 8 female pupil, severe hearing loss, oral)

"There's actually a couple of posters about, telling people to, like, t-a-l-k l-i-k-e t-h-i-s and I don't really like it when people do that. Usually I try to not laugh because it's usually the really stupid people who do that. I mean I haven't had it for like a year now" (Year 9 female pupil, profound hearing loss, cochlear implant, oral)

"Some of our hearing friends understand that we don't want to be any different but then people who are kind of friends just make us different somehow" (Year 8 male pupil, severe hearing loss, oral)

"Some bloke is horrible, he's not interested in deaf, respect for deaf" (Year 8 male pupil, profound hearing loss, signing)

Interacting with deaf people

As illustrated in Chapter 3, 18 out of the 25 schools visited, had a Hearing Impaired Unit or a Special Educational Needs Base. The pupils in these schools had the experience of being in a mainstream school whilst having other deaf pupils around them. They were asked what it was like to have other deaf pupils in the school and whether their interactions with deaf pupils differed from those with hearing pupils.

What deaf pupils say

Most pupils agree that having other deaf pupils around has distinct advantages:

- they feel they are not the only ones with a hearing loss
- they can talk to someone who understands them
- communication is easier

However, they also say that they like having both deaf and hearing pupils around them because:

- hearing pupils have different interests
- it helps hearing pupils understand deaf pupils and vice versa

"It's better than my primary school. There are more people like me." (Year 7 male pupil, severe hearing loss, oral)

"Like, you see, we've all got hearing problems so it's not just one person that's sort of left out. It's all of us and we learn from each other different things." (Year 9 male pupil, moderate hearing loss, oral)

"With hearing I don't understand them but I understand deaf friends better. With deaf and some hearing pupils because we know what we talk about in sign language ..." "I feel I need deaf friends. If a person is alone, they will get bullied. It is safer to be with friends." (Year 7 female pupil, profound hearing loss, cochlear implant, signing)

"We can talk about things, we're the same ... It's much easier to talk to my friends who are hearing impaired here" (Year 9 female pupil, severe hearing loss, signing)

"There's a lot of other deaf people that I can speak to." (Year 9 female pupil, moderate hearing loss, oral)

"I'm interested in children who are deaf. I like that ... I like deaf and hearing mixing because when deaf people need more than lipreading I understand. I believe that I want hearing and deaf, I try to make clear my lips but if they don't understand what I'm saying I can sign to them but I like to lipread so hearing children understand me." (Year 7 female pupil, profound hearing loss, signing)

"I think it's good to have friends who can hear, then it might help you understand other people apart from deaf children and stuff." (Year 7 female pupil, severe hearing loss, oral)

"It is good that it is mixed here, you can have more friends. Deaf pupils can teach hearing to sign and hearing pupils can teach deaf to speak. It will help for the future when you work with hearing or going out with hearing friends." (Year 8 male pupil, profound hearing loss, signing)

Hearing pupils' perspectives

The hearing pupils interviewed see the deaf pupils as their friends and classmates and are reluctant to use any label to describe their hearing loss. Nevertheless, they know who the deaf pupils are because of their hearing aids, radio aids, because teachers point them out or because they attend the Hearing Impaired Unit.

They realise that deafness affects the lives of their deaf friends when interacting with both hearing pupils and teachers. They also highlight the importance, for a deaf pupil, of having other deaf pupils around the school.

Their views on the academic and social inclusion of deaf pupils are presented in more detail in Chapters 6 and 7.

"I'm best friends with two people that wear hearing aids and I just call them by their names." (Year 7 female pupil)

"I would say deaf or hearing impaired, something like that…" (Year 8 female pupil)

"No, we just call them by their names" (Year 8 male pupil)

"Well, I'd just say he wears a hearing aid, but it doesn't really stop him in any way. He still uses his brain!" (Year 8 male pupil)

"They all went into the same room as him." (Year 9 male pupil)

"They're the same but they're different as well because they can't hear and they need someone else to tell them what to do and stuff, instead than just telling them straight." (Year 7 female pupil)

"He doesn't like people fussing over him, he just wants to be treated like a normal person, although sometimes it doesn't happen." (Year 8 male pupil)

"It depends really, because if you know how to sign and you know how they want you to communicate, then it's quite the same but if you don't, it would be quite different." (Year 8 female pupil)

"He's deaf and everyone else is hearing. Not many people know sign language so can't communicate, make friends or anything." (Year 8 male pupil)

"Treat them just like you treat your friends with hearing, not differently, just pay attention a little bit how you speak to them." (Year 7 female pupil – advice to hearing puppets)

"I've learnt to be calm, really patient, and say things again and again, so I learnt to be patient." (Year 9 male pupil)

"Well, it's just the way they talk to us compared to him, so much difference until obviously he gets it across he doesn't need it and then it just collapses.

"It's weird, very weird, because they just suddenly change from being really mean to really kind to him."

"Yeah, it just makes you feel very envious, jealous, when he gets into trouble, he can just get out of it by fiddling with his hearing aid!" (2 Year 8 male pupils)

"Because you want to talk to someone who is deaf, it doesn't matter if they know sign language, you want someone who knows what you're going through, how you're feeling. It's alright for us because there's lots of hearing people, but for them to approach others is different really because, if there's a group of deaf people, there's nothing to be worried about, like a back up. They can go, turn around and talk to deaf people. Because I doubt that the deaf students will come to us, we have to approach them, they would never approach us." (Year 8 female pupil)

"If it's only one person in the whole entire school who has a hearing aid, that person is, like, left out. He or she might say things like 'Oh why am I the only one? Why am I like this?' It's like they start to get upset about who they are because they are the only one that needs a hearing aid. If there's the whole school, then people with hearing might not really care much because there's only one person. But if there's more people they might pay more attention." (Year 9 female pupil)

Chapter 5

School ethos

School ethos

Introduction

The discussion with pupils about their experiences of inclusion revealed various aspects of the school ethos, such as whether diversity is valued in their school, communication practices, level of deaf awareness, equal opportunities policies and withdrawal from mainstream activities. The information detailed in this chapter reflects pupils' views, which are not necessarily the same as their schools'.

Figure 9 illustrates how the threads emerging from the data relate to the topic of school ethos. The symbol == means 'is associated with', whilst [ ] means 'is part of'.

Figure 9 Data on School Ethos

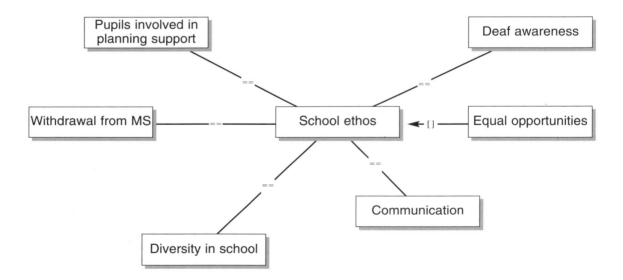

Valuing diversity in school

The ethos of the school was identified as a key aspect of effective inclusion in RNID's *A Review of Good Practice in Deaf Education*. While this is hard to define, it includes the attitudes of staff and pupils to difference and to valuing everyone.

The majority of pupils interviewed describe their school in positive terms and are aware of the school's attitude towards their deafness. Valuing diversity also seems to decrease the likelihood of being teased or bullied by other pupils.

Examples of practical initiatives appreciated by the pupils, in relation to valuing diversity are:

- homework clubs for all pupils

- sign language clubs for both deaf and hearing pupils

- peer support

- counselling

Unfortunately a small number of pupils have had some negative experiences, such as being excluded from school trips because of their hearing loss or having to follow different rules compared to hearing pupils.

What the pupils say about their positive experiences

"I'm quite happy where I am now... There's nothing to be ashamed of, being deaf in this school." (Year 9 female pupil, moderate hearing loss, signing)

"I like the way they can arrange stuff like this to happen so, like, they don't just treat me like, 'oh, I'm another person'. They don't just say, 'oh, you're deaf', whatever, 'you can carry on'. They actually say you can come up here and you can talk to someone about it. I'm treated a bit more than other people are, which I don't think it's very fair but it's still quite good for me. They're not just acknowledging me like another person, they get to arrange other things for me and stuff. Good special needs arrangements." (Year 7, moderate hearing loss, oral)

"I would say it was alright because you make friends really easily and you wouldn't get picked on for being hard of hearing or anything and the teachers aren't mean to you." (Year 8 female pupil, moderate hearing loss, oral)

"They just dealt with it, when someone called me 'that thing', they dealt with it. [In primary school] they said, 'oh, just ignore them and it'll go away'. When they deal with it [teasing and name calling], it doesn't happen again." (Year 7 male pupil, severe hearing loss, oral)

"They are very understandable. They don't mind repeating things for me, they're not rude, they don't take the mickey out of me or anything. Like I said, they're very understandable" (Year 7 male pupil, moderate hearing loss, oral)

"I'd tell him that the teachers have got good deaf awareness and will listen to you all the time and, if you have any problem, you can always talk about it and teachers always help and stop trouble." (Year 8 male pupil, profound hearing loss, signing)

"In every year there's someone with a hearing loss so they're all like… All teachers understand, they all help and stuff like that." (Year 9 male pupil, severe hearing loss, oral)

"Some kids might just say, 'oh, you're deaf!' whatever but, apart from that, it's alright." (Year 7, moderate hearing loss, oral)

"Some hearing pupils do bully deaf pupils. Hearing pupils think that deaf pupils should be in a different school but the head teacher here is happy having deaf pupils coming to this school." (Year 9 male pupil, profound hearing loss, cochlear implant, signing)

"Lots of people come to the homework club. I've only been once but it's alright. It's for anybody who needs help." (Year 8 female pupil, severe hearing loss, oral)

"I help out with the peer-support group here, because we've got a scheme that anyone can come up and talk to us if there's something wrong." (Year 9 female pupil, moderate hearing loss, oral)

"Don't be nervous because everyone is friendly around here. If you need help all you need to do is just ask the teachers or someone in the unit because they'll be happy to help you. There's always the support group that you can go to if you've got a problem or something." (Year 7 female pupil, severe hearing loss, oral – advice given to deaf puppet)

"Sometime we go with Miss, it's a bit like a therapy thingy, where you start discussing your feelings and that." (Year 7 male pupil, moderate hearing loss, oral)

"In Year 7, in PSE, we do this special hearing thing where they [the hearing pupils] get taught about it and they do things like try out radio aids in the science lesson so they understand about it." (Year 8 female pupil, severe hearing loss, oral)

"I remember once, the unit teacher invited everybody, well not everybody but some classes and we had a discussion, well, she talked to hearing people about deafness. I do think that helps and some people came up and said hello after that lesson." (Year 8 male pupil, severe hearing loss, oral)

"At hearing impaired week we also learnt a bit more about how they feel and their senses." (Year 9 female pupil, hearing)

What the pupils say about their negative experiences

"Sometimes teachers don't let deaf pupils go to the shops. I wondered why about this.

Teachers do let hearing pupils go to the shops. They would not allow me and I don't know why. It is not balanced, allowing hearing pupils to go to the shops and not allowing deaf pupils. There are big shops over there but deaf pupils are not allowed. We are not happy about it." (Year 9 female pupil, profound hearing loss, signing)

"I couldn't go [on the school trip] because the man might give us instructions like how far to go [in the water] and without my hearing aids on I wouldn't understand it." (Year 7 female pupil, moderate hearing loss, oral)

Communication

The approach taken to communication within a school context is one defining aspect of its provision. Approaches are generally described as bilingual (British Sign Language and English), oral/aural (with an emphasis on listening and speaking) or Total Communication. Definitions of the latter vary and may include the use of BSL as well as a form of sign in English word order. Definitions of communication approaches vary; similar practices are described in different ways and the same label is often given to very different forms of communication.

The schools visited seemed to be flexible in their approach to communication: they usually adopted a main mode of communication, that is oral/aural or signing, but did not exclude the other. For example, oral units also had sign language clubs, whilst signing units actively encouraged the use of equipment in classes, such as hearing and radio aids. A few units supported both signing and oral pupils.

In their responses, some pupils comment that the type and level of communication support is not always appropriate and/or adequate, especially when their preferred mode of communication is signing.

Overall, the pupils interviewed have had both positive and negative experiences when communicating with pupils and teachers and the majority of pupils enjoy communicating with both deaf and hearing people. A few examples are given here but more specific ones will be discussed in Chapters 7 and 8, which address academic and social inclusion.

What pupils say

"There's one [sign language club] on Thursday that just me and my friend [another deaf pupil] go to. The classes are quite fun; she does teach us some signs and things like that." (Year 7 male pupil, severe hearing loss, oral)

"Some people in school can sign a bit and some of them want me to help them to sign so it could be easy communication for me. Only the teacher of the deaf signs [amongst the staff]. My dad and my mom are deaf, my brother is deaf and all my friends are deaf. My mom can oral and sign, my dad can't talk." (Year 8 male pupil, profound hearing loss, signing at home, mostly oral at school)

"School is good, staff are patient. I found it difficult to use speech marks, exclamation marks and so on before I came to this school because I use BSL but I have learnt them here." (Year 9 female pupil, profound hearing loss, signing)

"I didn't sign before I came to this school. I learnt to sign when I was in Year 7. I didn't understand the other pupils' signing so the teachers had to help me. I go to Youth Club and use signing there and now I teach some to my hearing friends who I speak with also. My friends can sign for me when I can't understand speech." (Year 9 female pupil, severe hearing loss, signing)

"I would tell them that school is horrible and pointless. People will mess about and they would need more support at school. Good support would mean that they will get to learn lots of things and learn more. They may become uninterested if they don't have good support. Teachers should sign fluently." (Year 9 female pupil, profound hearing loss, signing – advice given to deaf puppet)

"I'm confident! I talk to both deaf and hearing people." (Year 9 male pupil, profound hearing loss, signing)

"Sometimes they [hearing people] don't understand. Well, not exactly what it means [to be deaf] but that you can't hear them." (Year 8 male pupil, moderate hearing loss, oral)

"I like communication with hearing." (Year 8 female pupil, severe hearing loss, signing)

"You're alone [in mainstream classes]. Others can listen to the teachers." (Year 8 male pupil, profound hearing loss, signing)

"In school I find work interesting and brilliant and I'm happy to mingle with hearing. I enjoy teaching hearing how to sign." (Year 9 female pupil, profound hearing loss, signing)

"I would explain how difficult it is for deaf pupil to go to school as she would get nervous and that she gets calmer later in the day. And how difficult it is for her to learn the teachers' names." (Year 9 female pupil, profound hearing loss, signing – advice given to deaf puppet)

"I like signing. I can learn and know what you are talking about." (Year 9 male pupil, profound hearing loss, cochlear implant, signing)

"I wish all schools mixed deaf and hearing. My mom thinks about that I would go to my brother's and sister's school but no, they're all hearing. There are so many hearing schools and few deaf and hearing mixing, very few, and we need many schools that are a mixture of deaf and hearing, ideally I would like every school!" (Year 7 female pupil, profound hearing loss, signing)

Deaf awareness

Deaf pupils have specific needs in relation to communication which must be understood by both peers and staff. Knowledge of cultural aspects of deafness and the contributions of deaf people to society can help to develop positive attitudes rather than a deficit model. A key issue will be how deaf awareness is developed throughout the whole school. Is it part of in-service training for all staff? How are peers informed? To what extent are deaf pupils part of the decision-making process in relation to how this awareness-raising takes place?

The level of deaf awareness of both staff and hearing pupils varies greatly. According to the pupils interviewed, some teachers show care and attention towards them, whilst others do not seem to appreciate the full impact of deafness.

Supply teachers and new learning support assistants (LSAs) are seen as having no particular awareness of the issues faced by deaf pupils and no understanding of the equipment they use in school, such as radio aids.

Some teachers, on the other hand, are very sympathetic and are aware of how stressful school can be for some deaf pupils, especially when communication with other pupils is problematic.

Some hearing pupils receive deaf awareness training as part of their school activities but each school seems to have a different approach to this issue and not all schools seem to provide such training, especially if there is no Hearing Impaired Unit or SEN base in the school.

Some deaf pupils are not entirely comfortable with information about deafness being made available to hearing pupils, whilst hearing pupils are glad to have such information. Two groups of deaf pupils suggested that it would be preferable for the information not to be related to themselves and their circumstances but to be about deafness in general. They also do not like being pointed out by teachers to the whole class or school but prefer to discuss their deafness only with their friends.

What pupils say about teachers

"He [one of favourite mainstream teachers] takes off the mike if he's shouting at someone." (Year 7 male pupil, severe hearing loss, oral)

"If I'm fed up or something. If I'm having a bad day and I've been badly abused or something, they understand that. If I don't want to do any work and they make it easier for me. I'd say that's good and they understand if I can't do work or something, if it's too difficult for me. Some of them do." (Year 8 female pupil, severe hearing loss, oral)

"When you have the transmitter on, if someone does something wrong, the teacher blasts out in your ear. You get an earache!" (Year 8 male pupil, moderate hearing loss, oral)

"It might be that they have taken someone outside to tell them off and they don't want me hearing it and then they just forget to turn the radio aid back on. You know, they just forget. It's not that much of a problem because I can still hear them." (Year 9 female pupil, profound hearing loss, cochlear implant, oral)

"When he's finished talking he takes it off, then he starts talking again and we keep giving him the microphone and he keeps taking it off every time. He'll start talking without putting it back on." (Year 8 female pupil, moderate hearing loss, oral)

"Twice, in maths, the teacher said to me, 'Detention! You didn't listen.' But I said I didn't know and the hearing, they didn't listen but they never got detention. It's not fair." (Year 8 male pupil, profound hearing loss, signing)

"This teacher, if someone teases me, she tells them off but if I tease them she doesn't tell me off because she's got good deaf awareness. Also, if I sit there and something is in the way and I can't see what she is saying, she always moves to let me see her. She's always fair to me." (Year 9 male pupil, profound hearing loss, oral)

"The LSAs have good deaf awareness, but if a new support comes in it's bound to be difficult for a while but then you get used to it." (Year 8 male pupil, profound hearing loss, signing)

"Everybody used to pull them out [hearing aids connected to radio aid]. This teacher even pulled them out and he never said sorry or anything. He thought it was a stereo and it wasn't. ... In PSE [least favourite subject], lots of people scream and everything. When I shout out because pupils hurt my ears, the teacher tells me to stand outside and I shout, 'No!' because it wasn't me, it was the classroom screaming their heads off, but she just makes me stand outside." (Year 7, profound hearing loss, oral)

"Me and my friend were walking towards our room last year and the teacher came to us and said, 'take these out'. She didn't know they were hearing aids and she thought they were like little personal radios. So, sometimes, teachers take those out. They're really annoying sometimes. It got mistaken quite a lot for a personal stereo in Year 7." (Year 8 male pupil, severe hearing loss, oral)

"The communication support teacher often watches me talking with my classmate and I can't tell her not look otherwise I will upset her. She sometimes joins in by asking questions about whatever we talk about, which I don't like. I want her to look away." (Year 9 female pupil, profound hearing loss, signing)

"Ask the teacher, I mean tell them you've got a hearing loss and say that you need to sit near the front because they can help you easier." (Year 7 female pupil, moderate hearing loss, oral – advice given to deaf puppet)

"Most teachers have got used to it so they turn it [radio aid] off when they're shouting but other teachers, like supply teachers, say, 'Oh, I forgot about that!' " (Year 7 female pupil, moderate hearing loss, oral)

"Once, when we go to a mainstream class, we heard so much noise and we joined them [hearing pupils] by laughing. The class teacher picked us out and pull out of that class." (Year 9 male pupil, profound hearing loss, signing)

What pupils say about hearing pupils

"When I met them [hearing friends] the first time it was a bit awkward because they'd realise I'm a bit deaf and they might think it's dangerous, that I might give it to them, pass it on. I have to tell them that I can be mixed with hearing and it doesn't affect hearing people. The only difference would be that I might not be able to hear what you say but I can lipread you so other people are OK, some of them." (Year 8 male pupil, profound hearing loss, signing)

"Try not to say, 'what's that in your ear?' Don't try to offend them by saying, 'why can't you hear very well?' and stuff like that, because sometimes they find it offending. Just treat him like a normal human being." (Year 7 male pupil, moderate hearing loss, oral – advice given to hearing puppets)

What pupils say about information in schools

"Sometimes it's bad [to give information out to hearing pupils] because, for example, they say, 'Make sure you move your mouth' and that. Then some people would probably go around not moving their mouths when trying to speak about us." (Year 7 female pupil, severe hearing loss, oral)

"I prefer people to know [about deafness] because they speak more clearly." (Year 7, female pupil, profound hearing loss, oral)

"It would ruin everything, it would just ruin everything... Everyone would know and then it would talk about you and it just wouldn't feel right. You would like to have your friends, who you'd speak to every day at school and that and let them know what it's all about but you wouldn't want the whole school knowing 'cause it's just no point really, 'cause you're not going to speak to the whole school every day, are you? I think they should know about hearing loss and stuff but, personally, I wouldn't really like one of them to know everything about me. It's really embarrassing 'cause sometimes teachers tend to go, 'oh, can you be quiet, we've got deaf children in the class!' and how you should be quiet and shouldn't be noisy otherwise they won't be able to hear and everything. And you're like, 'Why did you do that? You've just embarrassed me so much, why did you have to?' " (Year 8 female pupil, moderate hearing loss, oral)

"We learn more and we learn how they feel and how we make it easier for them." (Year 8 female pupil, hearing)

"Before I didn't know anyone who was deaf. If we ever meet anybody who's deaf again, we just know what to do and won't panic." (Year 9 male pupil, hearing)

Equal opportunities

The ethos of the school is often demonstrated by relationships between staff and between staff and pupils and will influence the content and delivery of the curriculum. Aspects of this are coded in some form of policy document, such as an equal opportunities document, which may be shared with pupils in different ways.

Most of the schools involved in the project had an information pack, which contained a statement on equal opportunities.

In the responses, only five out of the 39 pupils interviewed individually have an idea of what an equal opportunities policy is, but none seems to know whether their school has one.

34 pupils do not know what the expression means.

What the pupils say

"Is it something like people who have a hearing loss should have the same opportunities as people who don't have any hearing loss? *Interviewer:* Do you know if the school has one? *Pupil:* I don't think so. I don't think they do. I don't know." (Year 9 male pupil, moderate hearing loss, oral)

"A what? Oh yeah, like if someone is whatever they can do the same thing? *Interviewer*: Do you know if there's one in this school? *Pupil*: No, we don't really get excluded from anything, I think everyone can do similar things." (Year 9 female pupil, profound hearing loss, cochlear implant, oral)

"Yeah, it should have, I think. We've got a code of conduct." (Year 7 male pupil, moderate hearing loss, oral)

"What's that?" (Year 9 female pupil, severe hearing loss, oral)

"Yeah. We've got equal opportunities like in PHSE, that's one of the things we do and we have to do this activity and it said all these things and you have to put them into a column if they were just for men, just for women or both and all of them were both and that helped us understand you can do anything." (Year 8 female pupil, moderate hearing loss, oral)

"Yeah, I heard of it, is it to help disabled people or something? *Interviewer*: Is there one in the school? *Pupil*: I don't think so, I'm not sure." (Year 9 female pupil, moderate hearing loss, oral)

Withdrawal from mainstream

Pupils may be withdrawn from the classroom for pre-tutoring of a particular concept or aspect of the curriculum or to follow up something taught in an earlier session. They may also work on specific aspects of the curriculum in a small group. This can have the advantage of a better acoustic environment, more individual help, work undertaken at an appropriate level and in the case of pre-tutoring the opportunity for the pupil to access the subsequent mainstream lesson more effectively. Teachers may see this as a very effective means of support, but how do the deaf and hearing pupils perceive it?

Most pupils interviewed use Hearing Impaired Units or SEN bases for extra support; however, one quarter of the participants have some classes in the Unit, rather than in mainstream. The subjects taught in Units are, usually, English and Maths and, in some cases, Science. Most pupils see these classes as a bridge towards full-time inclusion, that is, as a way of catching up with their hearing peers.

Withdrawal from mainstream classes can sometimes be due to the lack of LSAs and Communication Support Workers.

Almost all the pupils take their tests or exams in the Unit or separately from their hearing classmates, particularly when listening to a tape is involved, for example for Modern Languages or Mental Arithmetic.

What pupils say

"If I'm really stuck on something like French or something, I do go there [the Unit] and Miss [the teacher of the deaf] helps me and then I get back to class but only do Maths in there." (Year 8 female pupil, severe hearing loss, oral)

"Some Maths classes are held in here, at the Unit. Maths is much harder than it is here in the unit." (Year 9 female pupil, severe hearing loss, signing)

"I have Maths and English here but next year I will join the mainstream classes instead." (Year 9 male pupil, profound hearing loss, cochlear implant, signing)

"I don't go to mainstream classes because I am not very good with English. As soon as I am I will go to mainstream class." (Year 7 male pupil, profound hearing loss, signing)

"I've got extra English instead of a foreign language." (Year 7 female pupil, moderate hearing loss, oral)

"The difference for me in English classes is that English here, at the Unit, we would concentrate on sentence construction, where in mainstream class they would study *Macbeth* or *Twelfth Night*. I found Shakespeare difficult because they read it out loud in class." (Year 7 female pupil, severe hearing loss, signing)

"I found it daunting when I began going to mainstream classes." (Year 9 female pupil, profound hearing loss, signing)

"When the interpreter is off sick, we ask the teacher permission to be excused and we come here to the Unit and the teacher here will supervise us while we work." (Year 9 male pupil, profound hearing loss, signing)

"I don't go to mainstream often because I would need an interpreter to follow what is being said." (Year 8 male pupil, profound hearing loss, signing)

"I feel differently [about tests] because I can't hear the speaker properly, because there's just one big speaker. So a lady comes in, in a room like this, and I sit here for the same amount of time." (Year 9 male pupil, profound hearing loss, oral)

"It's less distracting to have exams in the Unit because everyone else does them in the Sports Hall and it echoes and that." (Year 8 male pupil, moderate hearing loss, oral)

"For the tests they come into here so that they can get everything right, not get distracted by sounds, 'cause I know that hearing aids sometimes magnify the wrong sounds, so if somebody dropped a pencil, it sounds like somebody's crashed two cymbals together." (Year 9 male pupil, hearing)

Planning to meet pupils' needs

The planning process for identifying pupils' needs, sharing information with appropriate staff and providing the right level of support is vital. Planning and liaison opportunities have been identified as an important aspect of inclusion in *A Review of Good Practice in Deaf Education.* How do the pupils perceive this? To what extent are pupils involved in the planning and how do they contribute to decisions regarding their support needs?

Twelve of the pupils interviewed discuss their support needs with their teacher of the deaf or SEN coordinator, whilst the rest do not seem to be actively involved in planning how to meet their needs.

All pupils seem to be aware of the fact that they need to share the support available with other pupils and that this is one of the reasons why they might not always get their ideal level of support.

There also seems to be a mismatch between pupils' wishes and teachers' views when it comes to using equipment, such as radio aids in classes. Some pupils are not happy wearing a radio aid whilst teachers would like them to do so during all or most classes. Pupils' views on equipment will be presented in more detail in Chapter 7, as part of the discussion on Academic Inclusion.

What pupils say

"They [support staff] just come to most of the classes, the ones we do most activities in." (Year 7 male pupil, severe hearing loss, oral)

"They come to all the classes." (Year 7 female pupil, severe hearing loss, signing)

"The lady, the teacher of the deaf, picks them [classes to have support in] and I've a timetable." (Year 8 male pupil, profound hearing loss, signing)

"I used to see this person every week and I'd tell her what classes were hard and that. I told her what classes were hard and she said she would tell one of the teachers." (Year 8 male pupil, moderate hearing loss, oral)

"They [support staff] just come." (Year 8 female pupil, severe hearing loss, oral)

"I ask the teachers and they just come up and see if I'm alright." (Year 9 male pupil, profound hearing loss, oral)

"I do ask her [LSA] sometimes, maybe in Science, and she says she might because she doesn't only work with me, she works with some other students as well." (Year 7 male pupil, moderate hearing loss, oral)

"They [teacher of the deaf and support staff] decide what's best. Because there are so many people in the school, in the Unit, they split up the time about what lesson they go to." (Year 8 male pupil, severe hearing loss, oral)

"I have a radio aid, I know I'm meant to wear it but I never wear it anyway, anywhere but in Science and Maths. Some teachers are hassling me to wear it in assemblies but I won't because I don't listen in assemblies because it bores me." (Year 8 female pupil, severe hearing loss, oral)

"I wore radio aids in the past but one day I realised that there wasn't difference when I wore it. I decided not to use it at all and Miss [the teacher of the deaf] asked why I didn't wear it. I told her that it was broken but eventually told her that wasn't much difference." (Year 9 male pupil, profound hearing loss, signing)

"We say that we don't need it [radio aid] and then they [support staff] say, 'No, use it'. They make us wear it but it's just, well, we just don't want to wear it." (Year 8 male pupil, severe hearing loss, oral)

"They seem to think it's good [to wear a radio aid] and we try to sort of say we don't like wearing it and that but they don't seem to listen. They just think, 'Oh no, it's best for you to wear it. It's better for you to hear the teacher and stuff like that.' " (Year 7 female pupil, severe hearing loss, oral)

Chapter 6

Staff roles

Staff roles

Introduction

Another important factor explored during the research project was staff roles. A number of different professionals are likely to work with a deaf pupil. Teachers of the deaf may be based in the school or may visit on a peripatetic basis. Mainstream teachers take the responsibility for delivering class lessons and may be supported by a teacher of the deaf. This could involve team teaching in a variety of different ways. Teaching assistants often provide in-class support, while communication support workers provide support for signed communication. Deaf staff may have a particular role in supporting or teaching the pupils within the curriculum or with particular aspects of learning, such as BSL development. How do pupils perceive these staff roles?

Most of the pupils talked about teachers in a collective manner, not always distinguishing mainstream teachers from support staff or specialist staff, such as teachers of the deaf. Nevertheless, the different roles of these professionals took shape through the narratives of the pupils and it is to these roles that this chapter is dedicated.

None of the pupils talked about deaf staff in particular. The only distinction they seemed to make was between teachers who sign and teachers who don't. From the research team's observations only three of the schools visited employed deaf staff. However, other schools might have also employed deaf staff on a more casual basis. This is an issue which will be discussed in the final chapter.

Figure 10 provides an overview of the threads relevant to the thematic of staff roles. The symbol == means 'is associated with', whilst [ ] means 'is part of'.

Figure 10 Data on staff roles

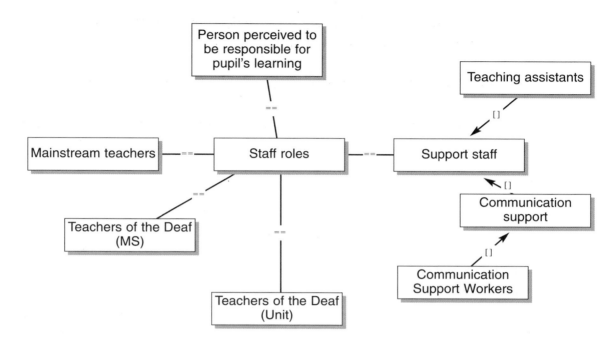

Person perceived to be responsible for pupils' learning

The pupils interviewed on a one-to-one basis were asked who, in their opinion, knew all of their grades and how well they were doing at school. Their responses are summarised in Figure 11.

Figure 11 Person perceived to be responsible for pupils' learning

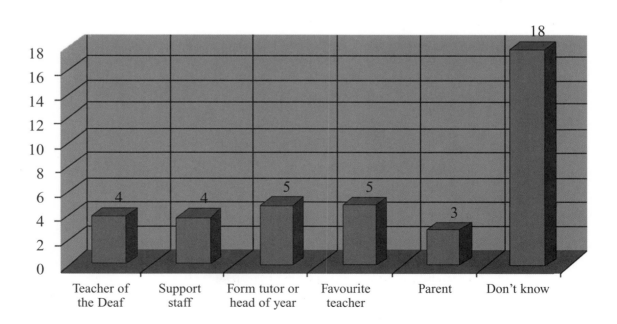

What pupils say

"It would probably be Miss [teacher of the deaf] or the support assistant." (Year 8 male pupil, profound hearing loss, signing)

"Probably my tutor." (Year 7 male pupil, moderate hearing loss, oral)

"The support teachers. They look always in the planner and everything." (Year 7 female pupil, severe hearing loss, signing)

"It would be the French teacher because she checks how you getting on and stuff like that." (Year 8 female pupil, severe hearing loss, oral)

"Could it be a parent? My mom. Most teachers know most of my results, grades and all that, but it's my mom, she's like… she wants to know what's wrong and advises me to get on with it and do my best." (Year 8 male pupil, moderate hearing loss, oral)

"My Science teacher because he's my Head of Year." (Year 9 male pupil, severe hearing loss, oral)

Mainstream teachers

All the pupils expressed a variety of opinions about mainstream teachers, as they seem to be the ones whom they interact with most of the time. They are seen as having both positive and negative roles, which often coexist side by side.

What pupils say

According to the pupils interviewed, the teachers' positive roles are:

- to facilitate access to the curriculum by
  - helping you when stuck
  - explaining things clearly
  - making sure you understand
  - being helpful
- to deal with other pupils when they
  - tease you
  - bully you
  - make too much noise in the classroom

- to understand you
- to be approachable

On the other hand, the negative roles are:
- to give you homework
- to have to help too many pupils
- to monitor your work and behaviour too closely

"When you're stuck on work, they come over and help you out." (Year 8 male pupil, moderate hearing loss, oral)

"The drama teacher always speaks clearly and it helps me understand and clear what I need to do." (Year 9 female pupil, profound hearing loss, signing)

"If you don't understand something, they explain everything to you again. Well, they don't explain everything but they give you what we need to know." (Year 9 male pupil, severe hearing loss, oral)

"I like the way teachers always make sure that you've understood things." (Year 7 male pupil, severe hearing loss, oral)

"If I don't know how to spell something, if I'm not sure what we're doing, stuff like that. If I can't hear something, they tell me what they said again." (Year 9 male pupil, severe hearing loss, oral)

"They help you with the work." (Year 7 female pupil, severe hearing loss, signing)

"My favourite teacher is Science. She's good at showing me books and pictures to help me understand." (Year 9 female pupil, profound hearing loss, signing)

"If somebody is behaving badly, he doesn't put up with it for long." (Year 7 male pupil, moderate hearing loss, oral)

"Some teachers are understanding… Understand that you don't understand something so that you didn't do your homework because you forgot some things." (Year 9 male pupil, moderate hearing loss, oral)

"The Maths teacher is good, he understands me." (Year 7 female, profound hearing loss, signing)

"If I'm having friends' trouble, one of my teachers tend to talk outside to sort it out and I find that quite good." (Year 8 female pupil, severe hearing loss, oral)

"What Miss does, she spends a lot of time discussing things with us, like, not just blabbing on. She's asking questions and hearing answers and, you know, what some teachers do is they just hear your answers but it goes in one ear and out the other. They like remember for three seconds but Miss remembers all that." (Year 7 female pupils, profound hearing loss, cochlear implant, signing)

"I remember in my old school I used to be too scared to ask the teacher about something but here I can, like, ask without them shouting at me and saying, 'You should be able to get this, we went over this three times!' " (Year 8 female pupil, moderate hearing loss, oral)

"They give you homework. They tell you off." (Year 7 female pupil, severe hearing loss, signing)

"If we put our hand up, there's usually a lot of other people waiting with their hands up already, like, we're waiting for a while." (Year 7 male pupil, moderate hearing loss, oral)

"He always look out for me to see what I was doing and, like I said earlier, I don't mind getting attention but he, like, gives too much. He's always got his eye on me so that's a bit annoying." (Year 7 male pupil, moderate hearing loss, oral)

Teachers of the deaf

The pupils interviewed, who were not part of a Hearing Impaired Unit or SEN base, did not seem to have a close rapport with their teacher of the deaf and commented very little on this role. Interestingly, those pupils who did attend a Hearing Impaired Unit or SEN base did not talk in much detail about the role of teacher of the deaf either. This could partly be due to the fact that pupils tend to speak about teachers in general, rather than differentiate between teachers of the deaf, helpers, mainstream teachers or communication support workers. Often the interviewer had to clarify which staff role was being discussed by asking additional questions.

What pupils say about peripatetic teachers of the deaf

The role of peripatetic teachers of the deaf seems to be, in the pupils' opinion:

- to support you in some lessons
- to assess your support needs
- to check equipment, such as hearing and radio aids
- to explain about deafness

"Miss [teacher of the deaf] comes with me to some lessons, like English, Maths, French and History." (Year 9 male pupil, moderate hearing loss, oral)

"I used to see this person every week and tell her what classes were hard and that." (Year 8 male pupil, moderate hearing loss, oral)

"I usually get check-ups when the teacher of the deaf comes and speaks to me about how I'm doing and whatever else. Last time she came, she brought a technician for the radio aids. They usually come around every two months or something." (Year 7 male pupil, moderate hearing loss, oral)

"She comes in every fortnight, just to check my hearing aids." (Year 7 female pupil, moderate hearing loss, oral)

"She comes in and she tests my hearing aids and asks how I get on in the school." (Year 9 male pupil, profound hearing loss, oral)

"I can't remember the last time I saw her at school. It was when I first got my hearing aid and last time I saw her was when I had the hearing aid tested to see if it worked. Last time she came in, she asked me how I was getting on with my hearing aid and a few questions like you're asking me now. Like how are you getting on with it and that." (Year 7 male pupil, moderate, oral)

"She helps me some time. We do work sometimes and she explains why we've got a hearing loss and, sometimes, she taught us about how the ear works." (Year 8 male pupil, moderate hearing loss, oral)

What pupils say about unit-based teachers of the deaf

The unit-based teachers of the deaf seem to be easy to communicate with and are attributed the following roles by pupils:

- to help and support you with
  - homework
  - tests and exams
  - revision
  - various subjects
- to assess support needs
- to coordinate support staff
- to be emotionally supportive

On a less positive note, the pupils remarked that, occasionally, teachers of the deaf could also be intrusive and interfere with their academic work and/or social life.

"They help me. Usually they help me go through tests, like revising and stuff. They want just to help me, they do, through work." (Year 8 female pupil, severe hearing loss, oral)

"The teacher of the deaf picks them [classes to have support in]." (Year 8 male pupil, profound hearing loss, signing)

"I prefer teachers here, at the Unit, than the mainstream teachers. Here they help me to understand the meaning. The mainstream teachers don't, they talk way too fast." (Year 7 male pupil, profound hearing loss, signing)

"I've had some problems with my friends and Miss is just a shoulder there. They're just like a teacher should be." (Year 8 female pupil, severe hearing loss, oral)

"She helps me if I have some problems, if I have a problem we talk." (Year 8 male pupil, profound hearing loss, signing)

"She came into Science once, when I was doing this big experiment with my friends and she was ruining the whole thing. She was just nagging us to get on with things and she wouldn't let us stop and talk for a minute." (Year 9 female pupil, profound hearing loss, oral)

"Sometimes we find the teacher a bit unfair because our hearing friends are not always allowed up here. She doesn't really like our friends, I don't know why." (Year 8 female pupil, severe hearing loss, oral)

Support staff

Either teaching assistants or communication support workers usually supported the pupils interviewed. The line between the two roles was often blurred and the pupils used various terms to refer to them, such as helpers, LSAs (learning support assistants), support teachers and communicators. Although the two roles were perceived to be similar, the pupils commented more extensively on the role of communicators than they did on that of teaching assistants.

What pupils say about teaching assistants

The positive aspects of the teaching assistant's role are, in the pupils' opinion:

- to help
  - understand mainstream teachers
  - with communication
- to encourage you to work
- to be available when needed

The negative aspects of this role seem to be:

- to over-explain things
- to be always there, even when not needed

"If you have an exercise where we had to listen to a recorder and stuff. I can't hear that well and I can't understand what they're saying. I need help to figure out what they're saying. Saying stuff from speech, like saying just the way you need it." (Year 8 male pupil, moderate hearing loss, oral)

"A lady comes with me and the teacher talks and if I missed it, she writes it down and then she helps me with the work." (Year 8 male pupil, profound hearing loss, signing)

"If I'm stuck, like on a question, she helps me out and gives me a little example of it. If I'm struggling she's there. If I've missed a word of what the teacher said or a word I didn't understand, then she'll be there, helping me." (Year 7 female pupil, moderate hearing loss, oral)

"If I have support with me they know what to do and they write all the notes of what to do and what the main subject is so that's a good thing." (Year 8 male pupil, profound hearing loss, oral)

"She gets me to work hard, as hard as I can." (Year 8 male pupil, moderate hearing loss, oral)

"They're OK, they're just there if I want to." (Year 9 male pupil, profound hearing loss, oral)

"Sometimes you're trying to work and they keep trying to chat or say, 'What are you doing?'

I wish we could just do our own work alone without anyone going, 'no, do that again please.' " (Year 7 and 8 pupils, severe and moderate hearing loss, oral)

"At school, helpers, in lessons, keep prodding me and asking me if I'm alright, that sort of thing, they try to do my work for me! I mean, I think if the LSAs get bored, they just try to help me; they don't like sitting there with nothing to do. The teachers, they've got a whole class so they tend to leave me alone but the LSAs are trying to help just me so I don't get a lot of peace." (Year 9 female pupil, profound hearing loss, oral)

"Some of them always help me so they can annoy you because you don't want them to help you a lot." (Year 8 male pupil, profound hearing loss, signing)

"I know this is a really rude thing to say but I've got to be totally honest, sometimes the support teacher can be really annoying, really annoying. You just want to be like everyone else, don't you? But, and do your work as well, then like you've got some support teacher nagging you… they sit next to you and they just talk to you, and asking you questions all the time and just get so fed up of it all." (Year 8 female pupil, severe hearing loss, oral)

What pupils say about communication support workers

The positive aspects of the communication support worker's role are, in the pupils' opinion, quite similar to those described above for teaching assistants, that is:

- to provide in-class support, such as:
  - notetaking
  - signing
  - helping you to understand

- to support you during tests and exams

- to be easy to communicate with

The negative aspects of this role seem to be:

- to help too much

- to be intrusive

Finally, if there are any difficulties between a pupil and a CSW, it can be difficult to solve this, as the pupil could be quite heavily dependent on him or her to communicate with other members of staff in the school.

"I have a communicator who comes from the Unit. We get help from her, like, when the tutor's speaking and we have to write notes. We find it hard to lipread her, so she does it for us. I mean we use her notes to do the work." (Year 7 female pupil, severe hearing loss, oral)

"This school is very helpful, I got a communicator help me to do some work. They help me with the subjects I don't understand." (Year 9 female pupil, moderate hearing loss, signing)

"They make sure I've understood and they help me with my work. Sometimes they sign if I don't understand something." (Year 7 male pupil, severe hearing loss, oral)

"One support tutor comes to a class and signs what the teacher is saying and helps out with my work." (Year 7 female pupil, severe hearing loss, signing)

"She is always with me in classes. She helps me by signing what the teachers say. She also helps when I have difficulty in writing." (Year 9 female pupil, profound hearing loss, signing)

"They can only help me with the reading [during tests]. They just tell me what it says, they read it out, try to help you a bit more and explain what the question is." (Year 7 female pupil, severe hearing loss, signing)

"I have interpreter in English classes but she only interprets when I'm stuck." (Year 9 female pupil, profound hearing loss, signing)

"I understand when communicators sign, because I don't understand the teachers. I prefer communicators, not teachers, in mainstream classes." (Year 9 female pupil, severe hearing loss, signing)

"It's more peaceful without any support [in some classes]." (Year 9 female pupil, profound hearing loss, signing)

"The communicator tends to forget that we are not children! She would take our work and check them to see if they are good. Sometimes she feels the need to explain everything when I understood before. Sometimes when I stop writing realising that I have made a mistake, she would leap to the rescue, asking if I wanted any help. Often I said no but she would push me aside and take my work to check. I wish I could conjure something that would freeze her at least for a few minutes!" (Year 8 male pupil, profound hearing loss, signing)

"I have been with this teacher for a long time and I had enough of her. Sometimes I like her but sometimes I don't. I want to tell her [the teacher of the deaf] but I'm scared that she would tell her. I don't know what to do." (Year 8 male pupil, profound hearing loss, signing)

Chapter 7

Academic inclusion

Academic inclusion

Introduction

The main aim of the project was, as stated in Chapter 3, to document the pupils' experiences of inclusion. These experiences can be further divided into those of academic and social inclusion. It is to the former that this chapter is dedicated. Academic inclusion comprises various aspects which are part of daily school life, such as communication with teachers, access to the curriculum, use of equipment, homework, and so on. These areas were discussed with the pupils interviewed and Figure 11 shows how the threads identified in the data, which emerged from such conversations, relate to the theme of academic inclusion. The symbol == means 'is associated with', whilst [ ] means 'is part of'.

Figure 11 – Data on Academic Inclusion

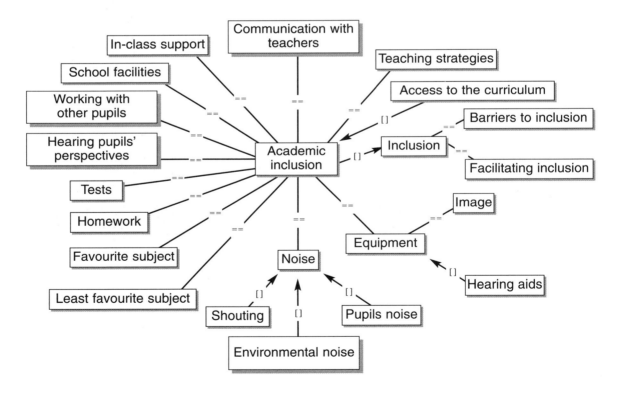

Access to the curriculum

Access to the curriculum is an essential ingredient of successful academic inclusion. It is also often what teachers consider to be of paramount importance when it comes to discussing deaf pupils and inclusion; yet it is not easily definable and it cannot be reduced into a simple formula.

The pupils interviewed identified factors that both facilitated or were a barrier to inclusion. Such factors illustrate the level and quality of access to the curriculum experienced by the participants. Other aspects that related to this issue were homework and tests and exams.

What pupils say about things that facilitate inclusion

In the pupils' opinion, active participation in and enjoyment of school activities are fostered by:

- clear communication
- teachers being understanding
- good deaf awareness amongst staff
- use of equipment, such as hearing and radio aids
- being open about deafness and asking for help
- friends supporting each other
- good school environment

"He doesn't shout a lot and repeat things again, helps you understand what it's about" (Year 7 male pupil, moderate hearing loss, oral)

"Teachers to sign [would be helpful]." (Year 8 male pupil, profound hearing loss, signing)

"The teacher actually speaking without using things, saying it, like exercises, speak out the exercises, not just put in a tape because recorded things are a bit hard to listen to." (Year 8 male pupil, moderate hearing loss, oral)

"If you don't understand, say so." (Year 7 female pupil, severe, oral)

"I'd say the teachers are here to help you, and any problem you have, you should come and tell them, like, if your hearing aid goes wrong and the teacher is always there to help you and fix it. And you should never be scared. Everyone feels scared when they come to school, not just deaf people, everyone. It's quite natural." (Year 9 male pupil, severe hearing loss, oral – advice given to puppets)

"Ask the teacher. I mean tell them you've got a hearing loss and say that you need to sit near the front because they can help you easier and everybody is really nice here, all the teachers are really nice." (Year 7 female pupil, moderate hearing loss, oral – advice given to deaf puppet)

"Just be yourself and don't hide back, don't back off sort of thing. Yeah, you might be deaf but no one is perfect. Just don't be quiet, be yourself and mix in with other people. In classes go to the front, not the back, so you can hear the teacher." (Year 9 male pupil, profound hearing loss, oral – advice given to deaf puppet)

"I've got this thing [radio aid]. You can plug it in anywhere and you can listen. The teacher is quite good, she always sits me in the front so I can hear." (Year 8 male pupil, profound hearing loss, signing)

"Use your hearing aids; it doesn't make much difference because people don't take that much notice of it here." (Year 7 male pupil, moderate hearing loss, oral – advice given to deaf puppet)

"My friends help me. If the helper is not there, my friends will help me." (Year 8 male pupil, profound hearing loss, signing)

"I think they should have bright buildings with lots of teachers around." (Year 9 male pupil, profound hearing loss, cochlear implant, signing)

What pupils say about barriers to inclusion

The pupils identified the following as obstacles to inclusion:

- poor communication
- lack of deaf awareness
- poor use of equipment by teachers
- lack of or insufficient support
- noise
- teachers not acknowledging your difficulties
- being socially excluded by peers

The last issue will be discussed in more detail in the following chapter, which focuses on social inclusion.

"He is terrible, he talks when he writes on the board. We always get to write a lot. Sometimes he writes questions on the board and I find it extremely hard to read his writing." (Year 9 female pupil, profound hearing loss, signing)

"Mainstream teachers speak too fast." (Year 7 male pupil, profound hearing loss, signing)

"Teachers who walk up and down like a tiger. You're trying to follow them but they don't stop, they just keep pacing round and everywhere." (Year 7 female pupil, severe hearing loss, oral)

"Sometimes she keeps the mike too far from the mouth." (Year 7 male pupil, severe hearing loss, oral)

"I was in Year 5, I should have been in Year 6 but, because there were no deaf children, only me, there was no signing person. I really wanted to be normal, to be in Year 6, it was not my problem. It was just me and they needed more children." (Year 7 female pupil, profound hearing loss, signing)

"It gets really noisy, it really annoys me so I get them [hearing aids] out." (Year 7 male pupil, moderate hearing loss, oral)

"Some teachers pick on me if I can't do the work or something. They just say that it's easy and I just need to jot it down or something!" (Year 8 female, severe hearing loss, oral)

"She doesn't take on board you're deaf." (Year 7 female pupil, severe hearing loss, oral)

"I'm not interested in school. Lots of people, hearing, they group all together and I'm left out." (Year 8 male, profound hearing loss, oral)

What pupils say about homework

The pupils do not seem to have any particular problems with homework, although most of them complain about the amount and level of it, especially when compared to their experiences of primary school. The pupils do not see this as being related to their hearing loss. As one pupil's quote aptly illustrates:

"I don't like it, but nobody does!"

The only thing that is problematic is that teachers do not always give clear instructions when assigning homework.

"The work is the right level. They do quite a lot of deep thinking. It's quite hard but it's, like, at my level." (Year 7 female pupil, severe hearing loss, oral)

"You get it everyday! Sometimes it's easy, sometimes it's difficult. We didn't get homework in primary school." (Year 7 female pupil, severe hearing loss, signing)

"I don't like homework. When I've been here all day and then I go back home, I want to have a rest. School's for work, home's for play so homework is not fair." (Year 8 male, profound hearing loss, oral)

"I always forget what I am supposed to do. I don't understand the instructions and I end up asking teachers for help." (Year 9 female pupil, severe hearing loss, signing)

What pupils say about tests and exams

Overall, tests and exams are not seen as a problem, except for the use of tapes. Some pupils find exams difficult because support staff cannot help as much as in the classroom.

The majority of pupils who are attached to Hearing Impaired Units and SEN bases usually take exams separately from their hearing peers in order to avoid noise and to aid concentration, as well as having special arrangements for dealing with tapes.

"They're OK. Sometimes they can a bit hard." (Year 7 male pupil, severe hearing loss, oral)

"They're easy, depending on the subject of course." (Year 9 male, moderate hearing loss, oral)

"I don't really like tests that much, I don't think anyone does" (Year 9 female pupil, moderate hearing loss, oral)

"It's hard because you have to think and it's just too hard because your support teacher can't help you or anything." (Year 7 female pupil, severe hearing loss, signing)

"One teacher used to give me the tapes so I could listen to it outside on the stereo, which I think was better actually. If I hadn't done that, it would have been on a tape player just in the middle of the classroom. But if I'm on my own, in a bit more of a quiet place and it's just right by my ears, that's better." (Year 9 female pupil, profound hearing loss, cochlear implant, oral)

"We usually come in this room [Unit] for a test because it's quiet and nobody can bother you." (Year 8 male pupil, profound hearing loss, signing)

Use of school facilities

Facilities available in schools, such as IT rooms and libraries, support pupils' academic activities, as well as enhance their learning experiences. Do deaf pupils take advantage of such facilities?

What pupils say

All the pupils interviewed know what facilities their school has, where they are located and, usually, use them. Some pupils report that their lack of, or limited use of, the facilities is due to the fact that these are often only open during break times.

Those pupils who are attached to a Hearing Impaired Unit or SEN base sometimes prefer using the facilities there because they are more easily available, for example there are not as many pupils competing to use the PC. Nevertheless, they also use mainstream facilities, such as the Library.

"I use the Library quite a lot actually because I like reading and I like playing about with the computers and stuff." (Year 7 female pupil, severe hearing loss, oral)

"I don't use the Library much but I use the IT room." (Year 9 male pupil, moderate hearing loss, oral)

"I use the Internet because it's free and you can go and get pictures for assignments or copy information. Sometimes I use the computer for homework, sometimes for games and homework." (Year 8 male pupil, profound hearing loss, signing)

"Sometimes I go to the Library to get books and you get this, I can't remember what it's called but it's just a sheet. When you've finished a book you have to write it down, like what it's called and what pages you've read. Then you colour one of the boxes and if it says 'reward' you get a present, like merits, pens, all sorts of stuff." (Year 7 female pupil, profound hearing loss, oral)

"I use the computers sometimes for research and stuff. Sometimes I go to the Library, just to get some interesting books out." (Year 9 female pupil, moderate hearing loss, oral)

"We have computer here [Unit]. We have Internet access. I work on the computer either in a mainstream class or in here. The Library is over there. I don't use it. I cannot be bothered. It's too far to walk!" (Year 9 female pupil, severe hearing loss, signing)

"We have computers in the mainstream school but I often use the one here, in the deaf Unit." (Year 9 male pupil, profound hearing loss, signing)

Noise

Environmental noise is a problem for hearing aid users and schools are often noisy, reverberant listening environments. Rooms are often large with shiny surfaces and windows; in certain subject rooms, equipment noise may also be an issue. Noise from other children involved in groupwork also makes listening difficult. Pupils commenting about noise may be referring to a level of conversation that could be seen as appropriate in a particular context but nevertheless affects hearing aid users, or it could be indicating that noise levels are not well controlled by the teacher. Shouting by teachers or other pupils can cause discomfort to hearing aid users as well as distort lip patterns, thereby making speech more difficult to understand.

What pupils say

The majority of pupils, regardless of their level of hearing loss, comment about noise interfering in their school lives. The main source of noise seems to be, in their opinion, either other pupils or the teachers shouting. The former usually causes the latter; hence a vicious circle is often created whereby pupils who use hearing and radio aids suffer in both situations.

Specific environments, such as gyms and labs, are also seen as problematic because of their acoustics.

"Teachers and people and noises in the class get me stressed." (Year 8 female pupil, severe hearing loss, oral)

"I turn my hearing aid volume to three, but I switch it off often in mainstream classes, there's too much noise." (Year 7 male pupil, profound hearing loss, signing)

"Mainstream classes are quite different, they can be very noisy, where it is very quiet here [in the Unit]. The noise makes me forget and find work confusing." (Year 9 male pupil, profound hearing loss, cochlear implant, signing)

"When I'm in background noise situations, like, well, classrooms when people are talking like with friends or something, I just can't hear the Miss and it can be a bit weird I suppose." (Year 9 female pupil, profound hearing loss, cochlear implant, oral)

"It does get a bit noisy sometimes. If I've got a headache, I won't wear my hearing aids." (Year 7 female pupil, moderate hearing loss, oral)

"This teacher is always angry and shouting in my radio aids. When he shouts my radio aid is hurting me." (Year 7 female pupil, profound hearing loss, signing)

"Some teachers are very strict and they shout. I find it painful to my ears with my hearing aids." (Year 9 female pupil, profound hearing loss, signing)

"I don't like it when teachers shout, it gets really noisy." (Year 7 female pupil, moderate hearing loss, oral)

"I prefer communicators, not teachers, in mainstream classes. They are always shouting. Shouting makes me feel embarrassed." (Year 9 female pupil, severe hearing loss, signing)

"Sometimes, they're shouting at one person and pointing at one person but it's in my ears, that's why I turn it [radio aid] off sometimes." (Year 9 male pupil, profound hearing loss, oral)

"I don't like it when I put the hearing aids on and someone shouts immediately after I've switched it on. It does hurt!" (Year 9 female pupil, profound hearing loss, signing)

"Some annoying people in the class know how to distract me, like by whistling. That really distracts me and I get really annoyed." (Year 8 female pupil, severe hearing loss, oral)

"There are some rooms where you might have difficulties – the technology rooms and some of the science clubs after school – because they have echoes and things like that and they're bigger, so it can be hard to see across the room." (Year 8 male pupil, severe hearing loss, oral)

"We've got a new sports hall, which is very big, very tall and it's got a wooden floor so you run along and it's quite noisy. It echoes a lot and the walls haven't been painted so there's noise." (Year 8 female pupil, moderate hearing loss, oral)

Equipment

All pupils involved in the project had either personal hearing aids or cochlear implants. In addition, most pupils had been issued with a personal FM (radio aid) system. Radio systems are designed to help with the problem of background noise and to allow the speaker's voice to be heard above other sounds. They usually require the teacher to have control of the transmitter and to pass it to other speakers as appropriate. While they can have clear audiological benefits, they are generally more noticeable than post aural aids and also require the transmitter to be handed to the teacher, something which pupils may find embarrassing. Additionally the effective use of the system requires the teacher to ensure that other pupils' contributions to lessons are repeated and that the teacher or the pupil takes responsibility for switching off the transmitter when it is not required.

What pupils say

All the pupils interviewed agree that equipment, such as radio aids, makes their hearing loss visible to others, which can be embarrassing. Those pupils who have had the opportunity to try digital hearing aids prefer them and like to wear them without using a radio aid. Teachers, however, insist that radio aids should be worn during classes, often contradicting the pupils' desire not to wear them.

Finally, the pupils see mainstream teachers' behaviour, in relation to the use of equipment, as erratic. Not all teachers seem to like to use, or know how to use, radio aids appropriately.

"I put it [radio aid] on but I don't necessarily turn it on." (Year 8 female pupil, severe hearing loss, oral)

"It helps but I'm a bit fed up because, sometimes, if I talk to other people, I can't hear what they're saying because I've got these on." (Year 7 female pupil, severe hearing loss, oral)

"When I first came here I had radio aids and they were annoying. I had to, like, get them out, bring them to the class and then give them back to the teacher and, if they were new, I'd have to explain how to use it and, you know, it was really annoying and it's another thing to carry around every day. Then I got new digital hearing aids and I found it was much better and I didn't think I needed them [radio aids] any more so I stopped using them. It's best to not have many things, which you actually have to wear and stuff." (Year 9 male pupil, moderate hearing loss, oral)

"In the first year, you just kind of don't want to hand it in, 'cause people aren't used to it but, in Year 8 and 9, people get used to it and they don't care. They just respect you for it to hand it in and then they know the disabilities you have." (Year 9 male pupil, profound hearing loss, oral)

"I've been trying not to wear it [radio aid] but my teachers make me wear it. I only tend to wear it when the support teacher's there or if my teacher knows I have to wear it, but I tend not to wear it if they're not there, 'cause it's really embarrassing getting it out in front of people, giving it to the teacher and you feel a bit weird and you just don't want to wear it." (Year 8 female pupil, moderate hearing loss, oral)

"Every year they [teachers in the Unit] do, like, a test with a radio aid and find out which one can hear better. And the results always come out as the radio aids but we don't feel the same about the radio aids, to wear them so, when the [support] teacher's not there, we sometimes don't give it in, because it's annoying to fuss." (Year 8 male pupil, severe hearing loss, oral)

"When they have to put the thing on, they have trouble getting that on. Some people just don't want to wear it. One of the teachers always says, 'Can I hold it up, please?' Because she doesn't want to wear it in her ear. I just hate when that happens. Some teachers make a big fuss of them, most of all the supply teachers because they don't know how to work it. They just leave it on their desk or something like that." (Year 7 male pupil, severe hearing loss, oral)

"Most of them pass the mike around the class. It's good when somebody is reading out or answering a question, then the teacher says it again because we're always at the front." (Year 8 female pupil, moderate hearing loss, oral)

Image

One's self image and how it is perceived by others is particularly important at this age. In Chapter 4 deafness and identity were discussed, but how does deafness affect the sense of self and image which go with being an adolescent?

The main concerns that the pupils interviewed seem to have in this area are:

- wearing equipment, such as radio and hearing aids, affects your image
- support and unit teachers treat you as a child
- if the teachers point you out as being deaf, it can be embarrassing.

"I suppose in secondary school, it's a lot about image but it [hearing aid] doesn't affect my image. My hair just hides it." (Year 8 female pupil, severe hearing loss, oral)

"It looks silly, doesn't it, you know, when you wear it [radio aid]. I hate it." (Year 7 female pupil, severe hearing loss, oral)

"It's really weird [wearing hearing aids] when I've got my glasses on as well." (Year 8 male pupil, moderate hearing loss, oral)

"If I do wear it [radio aid], I either pull it under my jumper or under my shirt. I never like to show it off, I never show it. I'm really, like, embarrassed about it." (Year 8 female pupil, severe hearing loss, oral)

"My [Unit] teacher, the other day, said she would give a sweet or biscuit to who finished early and behaved well throughout class. It happened four weeks ago! Really!" (Year 9 male pupil, profound hearing loss, signing)

"When we were sitting in a circle [during a mainstream class], we were all talking, including myself, and she [teacher] told everyone to be quiet. She started saying, 'You need to be quiet because we've got a deaf person.' After she finished, you get them all looking at you and you're like, 'erm.'" (Year 8 female pupil, severe hearing loss, oral)

"Once, in Year 7, we had to tell them [hearing pupils] all about our hearing aids and everything and I felt so humiliated. I felt so embarrassed about it." (Year 8 female pupil, moderate hearing loss, oral)

In-class support

Support for a pupil during a lesson may take place in a variety of ways. Teachers of the deaf may team teach with the mainstream teacher or may support individuals or small groups with particular aspects of work. Teaching assistants and communication support workers will support the deaf pupils in the class, but may also work with other pupils.

This helps to avoid the danger of over supporting an individual and of the deaf pupil being seen as the only pupil needing help. It also allows the person doing the support to have an understanding of the extent to which hearing pupils are accessing particular aspects of the curriculum.

What pupils say

The majority of pupils interviewed, who attend a school where there is a Hearing Impaired Unit or SEN base, receive some in-class support, as did many of the pupils in schools without specialist provisions.

The in-class support provided does not, usually, cover all lessons. Classes such as P.E., Art and Drama are often the ones where no support is provided. However, those pupils who most heavily rely on communication support, for example those who use signing as their preferred mode of communication, find that lack of support makes lessons harder to follow.

Five pupils have no in-class support. They had received some support in Year 7 but found that they no longer needed it.

"The teacher of the deaf comes with me to some lessons, like English, Maths, French and History." (Year 9 male pupil, moderate hearing loss, oral)

"We have a chart up there and Miss comes with me for the lessons I need." (Year 8 female pupil, severe hearing loss, oral)

"I do [get support], no matter what. I get them for Modern Foreign Languages, French and German, and I get Science and a few lessons like English." (Year 8 male pupil, moderate hearing loss, oral)

"Somebody comes with me and my friend and they sign but not all classes." (Year 7 male pupil, profound hearing loss, cochlear implant, signing)

"They don't come to every class, they just come to some classes." (Year 8 female pupil, severe hearing loss, oral)

"I don't really like French, I don't understand it. I have no communicators with me. It's quite hard. I get communicators twice a week and they help me a lot" (Year 9 female, moderate hearing loss, signing)

"I do go to mainstream classes. It's difficult because I can't follow all the times. I would prefer to go with an interpreter." (Year 7 female pupil, severe hearing loss, signing)

"No extra support. In Year 7 there was a teacher who sort of came around some time but there's other people so she saw them and helped me as well." (Year 9 male pupil, moderate hearing loss, oral)

"I did use it [Unit's Support Staff] quite a bit but I found that I didn't need it as much." (Year 8 male pupil, moderate hearing loss, oral)

Communication

Good communication between the teacher and the pupil is essential for curriculum access. A communication support worker may facilitate this, but pupils and teachers need to engage effectively. The quality of communication will be influenced by the teachers' attitudes to interacting with deaf pupils, by their knowledge of individual communication needs and by their skills in expressing themselves, listening, watching and monitoring comprehension. In Chapter 5 the deaf awareness of mainstream staff has been discussed, but what do pupils think about their communication with mainstream staff?

What pupils say

The pupils interviewed reveal a wide range of awareness and expertise amongst mainstream staff, when discussing their experiences of communication with teachers. However, they all agree that communication is vital for them, in order to fully understand the lessons. This is also apparent from the discussion on teaching strategies, presented in the next section of this chapter.

Some pupils prefer unit teachers to mainstream ones because communication with the former is often easier.

"My Spanish teacher is very nice. They make sure you understand the words, they say it over and over again and she plays games with them afterwards so it's fun." (Year 7 male pupil, severe hearing loss, oral)

"My French teacher talks too fast. Sometimes a lot of teachers talk too fast." (Year 8 female pupil, severe hearing loss, oral)

"I'm fed up when teachers move when they talk. I need to follow them! Often I tell them to go back to the front of the class but they still forget. I also hate it when they talk while they write on the blackboard." (Year 9 female pupil, profound hearing loss, signing)

"Sometimes they're good, they look at you when they're explaining things. Sometimes they just look at you but then sometimes they really just look at you for ages. And then you want them to look at someone else and then you won't feel a bit uncomfortable. They do it because they think, 'Oh, she's got to lipread me, 'cause she can't hear me' and stuff like that." (Year 8 female pupil, severe hearing loss, oral)

"Particular teachers that we have lessons with them, I say, always speak directly to them as well because it helps them." (Year 8 male pupil, moderate hearing loss, oral – advice given to deaf puppet)

"Mainstream classes are boring! They're always talking but it's all signing here [in Unit]." (Year 7 male pupil, profound hearing loss, signing)

Teaching strategies

Appropriate teaching strategies are a key issue for deaf pupils' access to the curriculum and are a focus for mainstream staff training. Training sessions often involve emphasising the importance of visible communication, time for the pupil to switch attention from material to speaker/signer and the need for visual support such as text, diagrams, pictures or objects. The identification of key vocabulary, a clear structure to the lesson and the role of the teacher or the teaching assistant in checking comprehension are seen as ways to facilitate access to lessons. Are some teachers preferred to others because of the interactive nature of the subject that they teach? What teaching strategies do pupils find to be helpful or unhelpful during lessons?

What pupils say about their favourite and least favourite subjects

Some subjects, like Maths, are equally liked or disliked by different pupils but, others, such as Art and Drama are liked by the majority of pupils, as illustrated in Figure 12. [Pupils were free to express their preference for more than one subject.]

The reasons given for liking or disliking a particular subject are usually linked to the teacher's way of presenting, with practical and interactive strategies being preferred by all the pupils interviewed. Subjects where there is a lot of discussion or the teacher talking tend to be disliked and considered boring, probably because of difficulties with communication. Noisy lessons are also listed among the least favourite subjects.

"Fun subjects are very easy and you do lots in them. And you can sit next to your friends and not at at table, stuff like Drama." (Year 9 female pupil, profound hearing loss, cochlear implant, oral)

"Maths is easy, there's no difficult language, it's just easy because it's just numbers." (Year 8 male pupil, profound hearing loss, signing)

"I'd probably say Music, we do a lot of practical." (Year 9 male pupil, severe hearing loss, oral)

"I love PE because there's no writing." (Year 8 male pupil, profound hearing loss, signing)

"English. I enjoy writing like fairy stories and things. We are studying *Macbeth* now for the SAT, it's quite boring because we're going over the same script again but it's really interesting when you actually know what the words actually mean. It's really exciting and fun because we do lots of fun things and Drama." (Year 9 female pupil, moderate hearing loss, oral)

"Art, it's relaxing when I draw." (Year 7 female pupil, profound hearing loss, cochlear implant, signing)

"I don't like PSE, it's just sitting around. I'm fed up, I don't like it." (Year 7 female pupil, profound hearing loss, signing)

"RE, it's just boring. We have to read this book and people, like, volunteer for reading and then, once you've read it, we have to copy some questions off the board and it's just boring really." (Year 9 male pupil, moderate hearing loss, oral)

"Maths is boring. The teacher just talks for about half an hour. It's boring and a bit tiring." (Year 8 male pupil, profound hearing loss, signing)

"German, because the language is difficult for me to understand and the teacher just talks. It's just a boring lesson and especially noisy." (Year 8 male pupil, profound hearing loss, oral)

"History. It's dull and it's so boring that I fall asleep halfway through. In History we do a lot of reading." (Year 9 male pupil, profound hearing loss, oral)

Figure 12 Subjects: deaf pupils' preferences

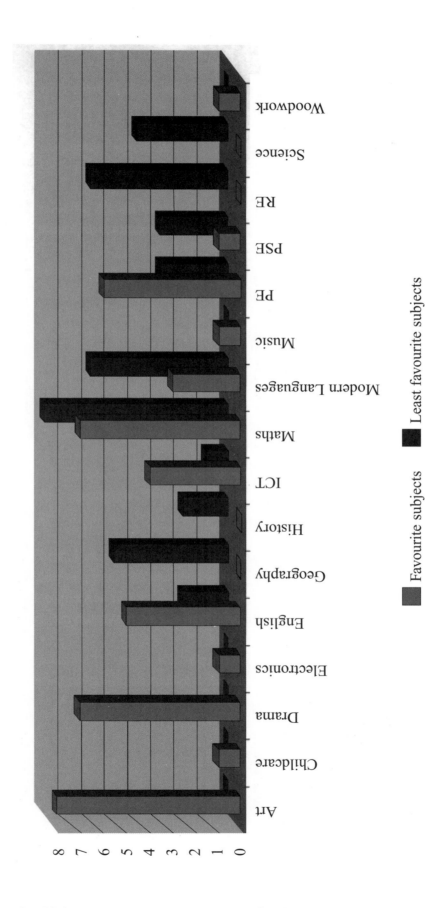

Favourite subjects   ■ Least favourite subjects

Figure 13 Helpful and unhelpful teaching strategies

Things that teachers do

- Too much talking
- Talk for too long about nothing
- Talk too fast
- Be too strict
- Not explain things enough
- Do not help me
- Makes work just copying out
- Sometimes when you need hope and other people need help they don't really help because a lot of people need help
- Shout too loud, cos hurt my ears
- Take the radio off
- Sometimes they don't repeat what they have said
- Can't understand when they speak sometimes
- Teacher turn their back in front of me and talking, I don't have a clue what she saying
- Just NOT LISTEN!

- They help you with your work
- Use videos and other funny ways of teaching
- Be understanding
- They help me if I need it
- Give you interesting work
- Giving me video notes or copies of tapes on listening tests
- Put me in front of class
- Repeat sentence again and again until I understand it
- Put my friend to sit next to me to help with work
- Give me a little bit of work
- They listen to you when you ask a question
- They explain about the work on the board first so you understand more
- Shout quiet
- Explain things again when I'm stuck
- When teachers speak clearly so I can understand

What pupils say about teaching strategies

Helpful strategies are:

- using practical activities

- using interactive activities

- making lessons fun

- providing clear explanations.

Unhelpful strategies are:

- talking too much

- not explaining things properly

- being boring.

Figure 13 provides an overview of what strategies the pupils seem to find helpful or unhelpful in the classroom.

"I like the way we do reading all together rather than doing it separately, so that we can do some work on it all together afterwards." (Year 7 male pupil, severe hearing loss, oral)

"Sometimes they show you how to do it if they are understanding. They show you how to do it or they show you how to do one, then you can do the rest using that. Some of them show you how they got the answer so you know." (Year 7 male pupil, moderate hearing loss, oral)

"In technology it's just good how we make to do things and design other things. It's like using your own opinion sort of thing." (Year 7 male pupil, moderate hearing loss, oral)

"A good lesson is when there's actually something to do. They make them more fun as work." (Year 8 female pupil, severe hearing loss, oral)

"Like Maths, sometimes you don't get to do anything, it's just him blabbing on about something." (Year 7 male pupil, moderate hearing loss, oral)

"He talks a lot but doesn't explain anything." (Year 8 male pupil, severe hearing loss, signing)

"They give you work sometimes and just don't explain it and you're sitting there stuck, trying to figure out what to do." (Year 9 female pupil, moderate hearing loss, oral)

"French it's boring because most people over in France speak English! The things we learn are just boring, it's too easy sometimes." (Year 9 male pupil, severe hearing loss, oral)

Working with other pupils

Work in the classroom frequently involves pairs or small groups of pupils collaborating. This is an important aspect of learning as sharing ideas and exploring topics together can increase understanding, knowledge and skills.

To what extent do hearing and deaf pupils work together and how do they deal with communication in this context?

What pupils say

The pupils interviewed think that working together with other pupils has the following advantages:

- sitting near friends makes lessons better and more fun

- you can help each other

Nevertheless, often teachers see pupils sitting next to their friends as a source of distraction and intervene to separate them.

For those pupils who prefer sign language as their mode of communication and for those who found lipreading difficult, groupwork can be an issue because of communication, so, for them, sitting near their friends, rather than any pupil, is even more important.

"They [hearing pupils] are all very nice. They care about you and make sure you've got your homework done OK." (Year 7 male pupil, severe hearing loss, oral)

"I can work better when I'm around my friends." (Year 9 female pupil, profound hearing loss, cochlear implant, oral)

"The boy sitting next to me and the girl, they're always silly. They make me laugh so it's really different, you know, a happy feeling that you're with your friends so I like that." (Year 9 male pupil, profound hearing loss, signing)

"You actually can make more friends [working in a group]. You're basically working and then you know what people are doing, their ideas and that. I find it easier in a group than working on my own." (Year 7 female pupil, moderate hearing loss, oral)

"Sometimes my friends tell me [what the teacher is saying] and they explain it as well." (Year 8 male pupil, moderate hearing loss, oral)

"I only see my best friend at break and one lesson every day. If I misunderstand something she'll help me, but sometimes she doesn't understand something so I'll help her." (Year 7 female pupil, moderate hearing loss, oral)

"They [teachers] give you seating plans, which is bad because you can't sit with your friends." (Year 7 female pupil, severe hearing loss, signing)

"It's easier to work with people who sign." (Year 8 male pupil, profound hearing loss, signing)

"If you work in a group or in English you read from a book, a sentence each, it's hard to hear them [hearing pupils]. Deaf people know they have to speak up but hearing people go mumble, mumble. Deaf people tend to speak up so that everyone can hear." (Year 8 female pupil, severe hearing loss, oral)

"Hearing classmates are not nice and I don't feel right. It would be better if I had my deaf friend with me. The teacher said she had to separate us. I was angry inside. She said she preferred if she separated us but I didn't like it." (Year 9 female pupil, profound hearing loss, signing)

Hearing pupils' perspectives

During the focus group discussions with the hearing pupils, some of the issues relevant to academic inclusion for deaf pupils were also discussed. It is to their opinions on academic inclusion that this section is dedicated.

What pupils say

Hearing pupils raise the following issues on the topic of academic inclusion:

- teachers can be both quite good but also quite bad when it comes to communication and deaf awareness; either has an impact on the deaf pupils

- noise during lessons can be an issue

- some teachers find equipment, such as radio aids, difficult to use

- teachers can over-help sometimes

Overall, the hearing pupils seem to think that the deaf pupils cope quite well with attending a mainstream school and that their deafness does not make too much of a difference in the classroom.

"It doesn't seem to make much difference really." (Year 8 male pupil)

"I think it's different because the teachers don't exactly know sign language and when they talk, they [deaf pupils] are always, like, turning around and asking, 'What's she saying?' Most of them don't understand what the teachers are saying and if there is no interpreter, then it makes it hard for them." (Year 8 female pupil)

"Sometimes she doesn't hear what the teacher says so the teacher that's helping her jots it down, shows it to her." (Year 8 female pupil)

"This teacher tries to communicate with them to tell them what to do and to tell them if they're doing right or wrong. I think he's the best teacher. He makes the deaf people laugh, that's all." (Year 7 female pupil)

"He's really as good, he's kind of better than me, actually! Sometimes, in English, a teacher's there to help him but he's really good." (Year 9 male pupil)

"All they can hear is probably the teacher and not everybody else talking [because of the radio aid]." (Year 7 female pupil)

"When the class is noisy and everything, they start messing about or start talking to themselves because they don't know what he's saying so they might as well talk to themselves." (Year 8 female pupil)

"Sometimes I think it's quite difficult [working in a group] because they can hear everybody else talking as well and they're just trying to block them out and just listen to you. Sometimes I can get the aid off the teachers and I can speak into that." (Year 9 female pupil)

"It's not easy [teachers using the radio aid]. Sometimes it takes a bit of time at the beginning of the lesson. Sometimes, especially the one in the ear, they can't get it on. Sometimes they just hold it." (Year 9 male pupil)

"I think, if they already know what they're doing, then they get it explained again, they just want to get on with it." (Year 8 female pupil)

Chapter 8

Social inclusion

Social inclusion

Introduction

The experience of school is not a merely academic one. The social aspect is vital, especially during adolescence. All the pupils interviewed talked about friendship extensively. When looking at the threads emerging from the data, friendship was the one with the largest number of quotations and when the pupils were asked to draw a mind map about positive and negative aspects of school, early on in the one-to-one interviews, they included a variety of aspects of social inclusion.

Figure 14 shows how the threads identified in the data, which emerged from discussing the social side of inclusion, relate to the theme of this chapter. The symbol == means 'is associated with', whilst [ ] means 'is part of'.

Figure 14 – Data on social inclusion

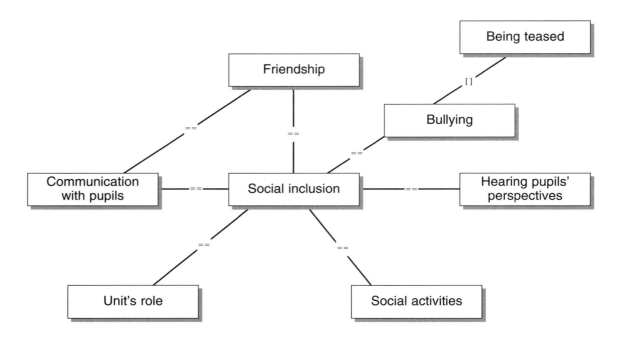

An overview of what positive and negative aspects of social inclusion were mentioned by the pupils in their mind maps can be seen in Figure 15.

Figure 15 Positive and negative aspects of social life at school

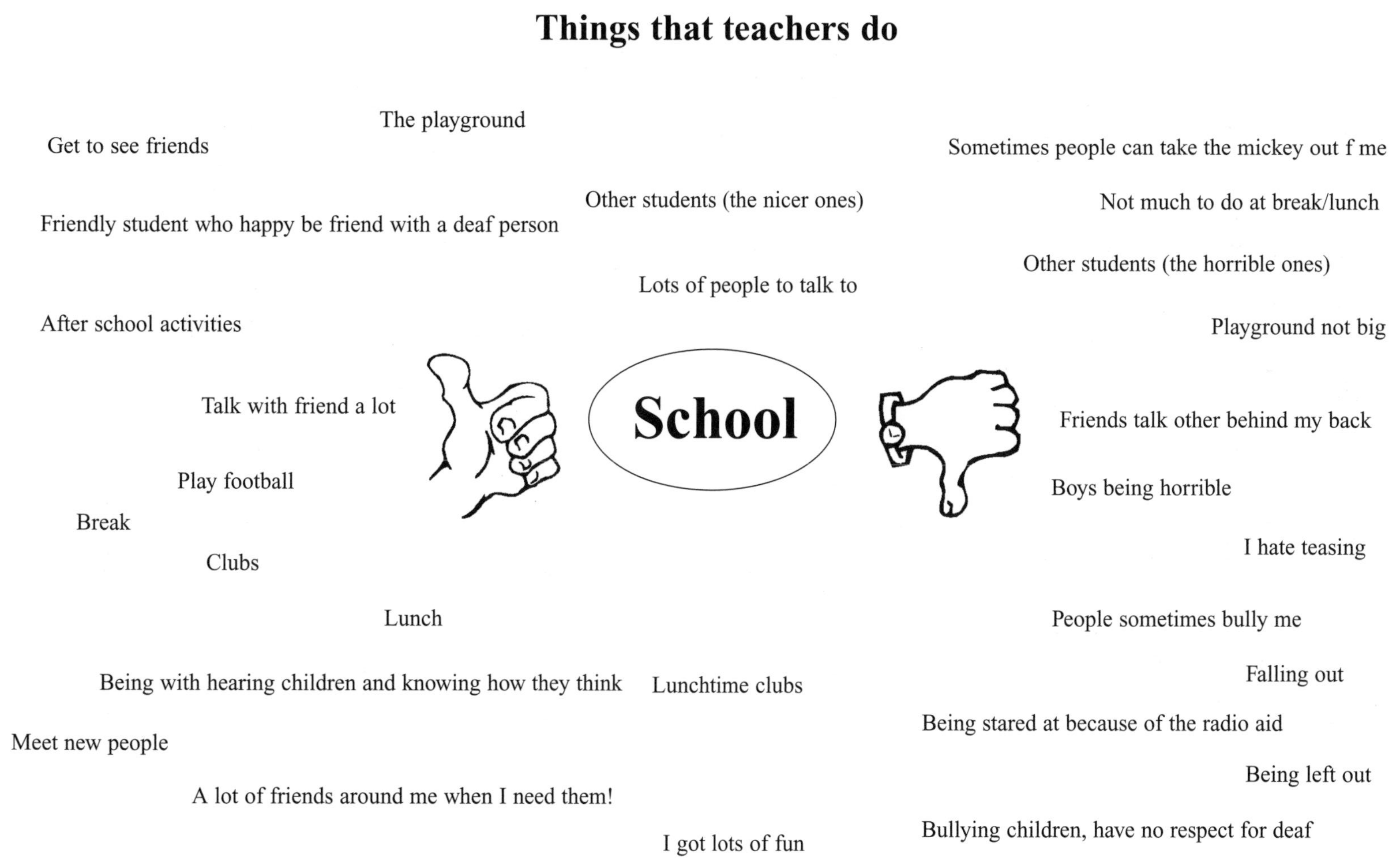

Things that teachers do

The playground

Sometimes people can take the mickey out f me

Not much to do at break/lunch

Other students (the nicer ones)

Other students (the horrible ones)

Friendly student who happy be friend with a deaf person

Lots of people to talk to

Playground not big

Friends talk other behind my back

After school activities

Boys being horrible

I hate teasing

Talk with friend a lot

People sometimes bully me

Falling out

Play football

Being stared at because of the radio aid

Being left out

Break

Clubs

Lunch

Bullying children, have no respect for deaf

Being with hearing children and knowing how they think   Lunchtime clubs

Meet new people

I got lots of fun

A lot of friends around me when I need them!

School

Friendship

Friendship is a significant aspect of life and peer relationships are a particular concern for pupils of this age. Relationships with other pupils are likely to be more significant to a child than relationships with adults in a school context. Being liked, being included in social activities and having identified friends in the classroom, playground and elsewhere is of major importance. To what extent do deaf pupils feel socially included?

What pupils say

As stated in the introduction, friendship is what the pupils interviewed talk about at length. During one of the first activities in the one-to-one interviews, 15 out of 39 pupils mentioned people and friends as what is most important to them in school.

Deaf pupils want to be treated as anyone else, yet they appreciate their friends understanding that they are deaf as well.

Communication can be an issue between deaf and hearing pupils, especially for those pupils who prefer signing. Another issue related to deafness is that it can be difficult, or even undesirable, to talk about it with friends, leaving both deaf pupils' and hearing pupils' questions unasked and unanswered.

"It's my mates that make me go through school. If I'm having a bad day, it's friends who talk to me about what I can do. Friends are the best thing." (Year 8 male pupil, moderate hearing loss, oral)

"I think it's a good thing to be with deaf people and hearing people because if you were all deaf people, then you'd all be into the same thing, like sign language and that, but if you're in a school like this, with hearing people, they can be different so it's good to be with different people who all like different things." (Year 7 female pupil, severe hearing loss, oral)

"It's a good school and everyone is kind. You'll make lots of friends." (Year 7 female pupil, severe hearing loss, signing – advice given to deaf puppet)

"No problem. I like both deaf and hearing. I have made lots of new friends and they're being very nice. I like sitting with them and it's nice to make new friends." (Year 7 male pupil, moderate hearing loss, oral)

"I have friends who are a bit like me, we've got lots of things in common and we just hang around with each other. We're completely loud we are, and we're into the same kind of things, like our favourite subjects are the same and stuff like that, our favourite teacher's the same, the kind of music, the same taste and stuff." (Year 8 female pupil, severe hearing loss, oral)

"They [other deaf pupils] have their own friends and I have mine and the thing is I don't really hang around people with hearing losses, 'cause I've always had hearing friends." (Year 9 female pupil, profound hearing loss, cochlear implant, oral)

"For me, it's a bit difficult to make friends because when they talk I can't hear them so they're not interested in talking to me, so it's a bit difficult. When I met them the first time, it was a bit awkward because they realised I'm a bit deaf and they might think it's dangerous, that I might give it to them, pass it on and I have to tell them that I can be mixed with hearing and it doesn't affect hearing people." (Year 8 male pupil, profound hearing loss, signing)

"All my friends, they treat me like one of them, like I'm not deaf but they do understand if, like, something happens. They do understand that I'm deaf and they know I can get bullied for it and they do back me up all the time, they do." (Year 8 female pupil, severe hearing loss, oral)

"Now they're like halfway in Year 8, they don't even care and they treat us like normal. We're just like hearing people to them, I think. They don't treat us like outcasts, they just treat us with respect and that's fine." (Year 8 male pupil, profound hearing loss, oral)

"Hearing are better off, they can hear and make friends with other hearing. Deaf only have to make do with few deaf friends." (Year 9 female pupil, profound hearing loss, signing)

"At first, talk to each other, kind of ignore that he's got a hearing aid, then ask him why he's got it, how long does he think he's gonna have it for, then just totally forget about it really" (Year 9 male pupil, severe hearing loss, oral – advice given to hearing puppets)

"Everyone says be yourself, that's how I made my friends. They didn't know, at the time, that I was deaf but I told them and they were OK" (Year 8 female pupil, moderate hearing loss, oral)

"One thing not to say is, 'What is that in your ear?' Because that's so annoying. I had that said to me about 50 times and it's just annoying. I don't mind it but I just don't like it." (Year 7 male pupil, moderate hearing loss, oral)

"It's just, it's something that you shouldn't talk about, you see. I mean I understand that they're concerned or something but it's something you really shouldn't talk about because you don't actually like being deaf, do you? I mean I'm OK with it because I've coped with it for all of my life now. I mean it's just something you really don't want to discuss. Is it good? Does it feel good? Is it contagious? Or something like that. I mean, I do get a bit annoyed if they do ask lots of questions. I say, 'I don't really want to talk about it. Do you mind if we just skip the conversation?'" (Year 8 female pupil, severe hearing loss, oral)

What deaf pupils do not ask or talk about with hearing pupils

For the final focus group activity, the deaf pupils were asked to write down on cut-out paper "speech bubbles" questions or comments they had previously felt unable to address to hearing pupils. Hearing pupils were asked to carry out a similar task. This activity emerged as a result of comments made during the one-to-one interviews. Some of the deaf pupils' comments are presented here, whilst the hearing pupils' comments are presented in the final section of this chapter.

Communication

Communication with peers takes place in an informal context, often in poor listening conditions and often in groups where it is difficult for the deaf pupil to switch attention quickly between speakers. Pupils may find that difficulties with speech intelligibility or lack of mutual signing skills lead to difficulties in understanding between deaf and hearing children. To what extent do deaf pupils perceive communication to be a barrier to social inclusion?

What pupils say

The majority of the deaf pupils interviewed recognise that communication with their hearing peers is not always easy, as it can be noticed from some of the quotations in the section about friendship.

Some pupils find that communication with other deaf pupils can be easier as they are more aware of appropriate strategies.

Time and familiarity are seen as helpful when it comes to communication.

"It's hard to make friends as it won't be easy to lipread them and they wouldn't know how to sign." (Year 9 female pupil, profound hearing loss, hearing)

"Here lots of people are hearing and don't want to speak to deaf people. Here lots of hearing people just say, 'I don't know what he's saying.'" (Year 8 male, profound hearing loss, oral)

"My teacher teaches them [hearing friends] signing and I teach them too." (Year 7 male pupil, profound hearing loss, signing)

"Sometimes boys talk with their head moving and I have to remind them that I'm deaf. They would cover their mouth, while they're talking." (Year 9 male pupil, profound hearing loss, signing)

"I used to go, 'I wish you'd speak slower' but that was some time ago, I don't do it anymore, I got used to it." (Year 9 male pupil, severe hearing loss, oral)

"It was hard because they didn't understand us at first but, after a while, they got used to how we talk and it was a lot easier." (Year 9 male pupil, profound hearing loss, oral)

"If they're not clear, then you have to tell them but, if they are, then you just leave it and carry on. A new girl came to our school and I made friends with her. At first, she didn't speak very clearly so I told her. It's alright now, sometimes I don't hear her but I just tell her and she'll repeat it." (Year 8 female pupil, moderate hearing loss, oral)

"Sometimes they talk really loudly and with their mouth, like, really open." (Year 9 male pupil, severe hearing loss, oral)

"With a group of hearing people talking, I feel left out. One girl signs for me but the others wouldn't wait and carry on talking. They say I talk like a baby." (Year 7 female pupil, profound hearing loss, signing)

"Sometimes when they say a joke and we don't hear it and they all start laughing and then they don't say the joke again. I do fake laughs. Sometimes I pretend I understand but then, to my best friend maybe, I might go and say, 'I didn't quite get that joke.'" (Year 7 female pupil, severe hearing loss, oral)

"Sometimes I can't get what they're talking about and I go, 'What are you talking about? And they go, 'Oh, I'll tell you later'. It makes me feel angry because I don't know what they're talking about!" (Year 9 male pupil, severe hearing loss, oral)

"If something goes wrong with the hearing aid and there's another deaf person there, then it's easy to explain to them what's wrong but they [hearing people] don't understand anything. Like, in free time, say someone says, 'Who wants to play football?' Sometimes you can't hear them and everyone else is playing and say we wanted to play football and we end up not being able to play or something like that." (Year 8 male pupil, moderate hearing loss, oral)

Social activities

After-school or break-time activities are an important part of the social life of a school. Do deaf pupils participate in these?

What pupils say

Most of the pupils who took part in the research undertake after-school activities, although some of these are external to the school itself, such as youth clubs or sports for example.

Eleven pupils state that they do not to take part in any organised activity, as they prefer to just 'hang out' with friends, play games or go into town.

Figure 16 summarises what type of activities the pupils interviewed engage in.

Figure 16 Type of social activities undertaken by deaf pupils

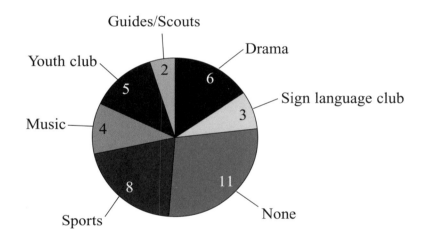

Role of the Unit

Eighteen schools included in the research project had units or resource bases; these bases had different titles, reflecting how their roles were identified by the staff involved. For example, an SEN base would be seen to support pupils with a range of special needs and the awareness of the needs of deaf pupils might or might not be different from that found in a dedicated resource for deaf pupils. Some bases were concerned not to be seen as a 'unit' in terms of being separate from the rest of the school and were never used for withdrawal purposes. In other cases, a unit was used frequently for withdrawal work or for social activities involving deaf pupils or deaf and hearing pupils.

How do pupils perceive the Unit in relation to their social life?

What pupils say

The Unit means that there are other deaf pupils around the school and it can be seen as a safe place, somewhere to relax and where communication is easier.

However, some pupils are also concerned that attending the Unit makes them more visible and can isolate them from other pupils.

"We can talk about things, we're the same. Like, in my primary school, people didn't really understand and it's much easier to talk to my friends who are hearing impaired here [in the Unit]." (Year 7 female pupil, severe hearing loss, oral)

"They see you as, 'Oh, she's just deaf as well' but in my old school they think 'Oh my God, she's deaf' and things like that and they think you'be really special in a way but here [Unit] you just get treated the same way." (Year 8 female pupil, moderate hearing loss, oral)

"With hearing I don't understand them but I understand deaf friends better. With deaf and some hearing pupils because we know what we talk about in Sign Language. I feel I need deaf friends. If a person is alone, they will get bullied. It is safer to be with friends." (Year 7 female pupil, profound hearing loss, cochlear implant, signing)

"I like to come here and relax. It's quiet here and I like to talk to my friends here. I prefer it here." (Year 9 female pupil, severe hearing loss, signing)

"We have a club as well, we're starting a Drama club in here [Unit]." (Year 7 female pupil, severe hearing loss, oral)

"Try not to shut yourself into the Unit because that's what the others do." (Year 9 female pupil, profound hearing loss, cochlear implant, oral)

Bullying and being teased

An aspect of relationships within a school context can include teasing, name-calling and other types of mental or physical bullying. To what extent do deaf children perceive themselves as being bullied or taking part in bullying behaviour? Do they see this as relating to their deafness?

What pupils say

Being teased and/or bullied can happen and has happened to some of the pupils who took part in this research. Schools seem to be aware of it and pupils think that, usually, staff members intervene when appropriate. Pupils are also sometimes prepared to confront those who tease and/or bully them.

These unpleasant aspects of school's social life are not seen as always being related to deafness, though. As one of the pupils says in a group interview: "There are morons in the world."

"Some people make fun of me because of the hearing aids." (Year 7 male pupil, moderate hearing loss, oral)

"You know how some people just blurt out anything but it's not all the time. You're just there and you probably caught them in a bad moment or something and they blurt out something but it's not really anything bad." (Year 9 female pupil, moderate hearing loss, oral)

"I don't like the hearing. The hearing tease me because I'm deaf. When they play, they stick together and if I want to join them they go, 'Oh no, not for you because you're deaf.'" (Year 8 male pupil, profound hearing loss, signing)

"Some see deafness as something funny and they can't stop laughing. They never bully me but they do other deaf pupils" (Year 9 male pupil, profound hearing loss, cochlear implant, signing)

"If they annoy you, first wait for a day or so but if it gets worse, tell the teachers and they'll sort it out. Be calm." (Year 9 male pupil, profound hearing loss, oral – advice given to deaf puppet)

"If someone calls me names I just ignore them, and if they carry on I start calling them names." (Year 8 male pupil, severe hearing loss, oral)

"When I first started this school, I got bullied a lot. One day in the playground they felt sorry for me in the end because I said to them, 'How would you like it if you were deaf and you're standing in the playground on your own. If you were deaf and I was normal I would be speaking to you!' They saw me crying in the end and they came over to me and said sorry. That was because I was the only girl in that year who was deaf." (Year 9 female pupil, moderate hearing loss, signing)

"They used to just swear at me all the time and start calling me names and stuff but I did say, one time, 'If you're picking on me because I'm deaf, then you can just stop now.' And they told me, 'No, we're not picking on you because you're deaf.' I think it got better since." (Year 8 female pupil, severe hearing loss, oral)

"People may be friendly or bullies but there's not much bullying, only from the older ones because we are smaller." (Year 8 male pupil, profound hearing loss, signing)

"I like doing those [homework in the Library or ICT room] at lunchtime because it stops me from being bullied and that and it gives me a bit more time to get my homework done." (Year 7 male pupil, moderate hearing loss, oral)

"At my primary school I had a mate and we used to cuss each other a lot, he used to say a lot of stuff about my deafness, but he had nothing else to say about me and I used to cuss him saying he's fat but as we got older he begin to get used to it and we just don't care any more. Everyone has at least a problem and if they don't really have a problem, the bullier would definitely pick out something to pick on them. They'll always find something." (Year 9 male pupil, severe hearing loss, oral)

Hearing pupils' perspectives

The hearing pupils interviewed during the focus group discussions had agreed to participate in this research project because they were already deaf aware and, for the most part, were friends of the deaf pupils interviewed separately. Nevertheless, they were conscious of what issues the deaf pupils face in relation to social inclusion.

What pupils say

The hearing pupils interviewed acknowledge that communication can be a barrier to social inclusion, especially when hearing people, both staff and pupils, cannot sign.

They realise that not everybody understands deafness as well as they do, and that deaf pupils can be the subject of derision and bullying, although they all agreed that the latter was rare. They also recognise that being teased and bullied can happen to anyone, not just deaf pupils.

"Sometimes it's difficult but, if you can't sign, you can spell the alphabet." (Year 8 female pupil)

"When they try to speak, can't always understand. They sometimes write it down as well and point at things. If you know them, you get accustomed to them and what they do and you, like, understand what they're doing because they've done it before." (Year 7 male pupil)

"If they ask you to repeat things, just because they didn't understand you, don't be rude. They're just like a normal person, really, just like everybody else. It's just that they've got hearing aids. You might have to repeat things a couple of time but, otherwise, they're just the same as you. Maybe speak a bit louder and look at them." (Year 9 male pupil – advice to hearing puppets)

"If they're in a group, he doesn't really know who's talking to him or not but when talking to each other he realises who's saying what and so he gets by." (Year 8 male pupil)

"They want to know what we're saying because we might talk about him, how stupid he is or something. Other people call deaf people 'deaf and dumb' and there's no need. They think they're different, like a handicapped person." (Year 8 female pupil)

"There's not exactly that much bullying because they don't exactly go up to them and say because if they did they wouldn't know what they're trying to say. So, usually, deaf people don't get bullied that much, unless it's inside the Deaf community where everyone is deaf, then maybe." (Year 8 female pupil)

"I thought, when I first saw her, that she might get some teasing but not that I know of, she's never been bullied in this school." (Year 9 female pupil)

"I think bullies just pick on people who are different to others, people who are, like, different race, different culture, different religion and they just put, like, hearing impaired people in that kind of group because they're different in a way as well." (Year 7 female pupil)

"Really most hearing people get bullied more than lots of hearing people because the person bullying, they're really scared of them because of the hearing aids and if they get damaged they have to pay a lot of money for it. But hearing people, they're normal so they haven't anything expensive to be broken." (Year 9 male pupil)

" I think it would be OK with everybody, there might be one or two troublemakers, that's all." (Year 8 male pupil)

What hearing pupils do not ask or talk about with deaf pupils

The hearing pupils used the speech bubbles to write down questions or statements which they had not had the courage to address to deaf pupils. Their statements conclude this chapter.

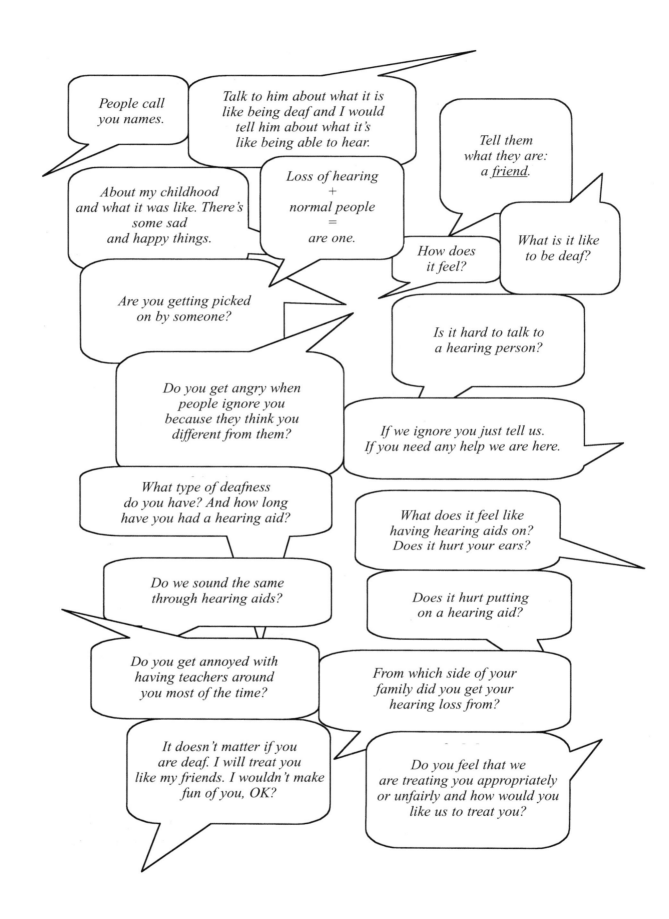

Chapter 9

Summary:
findings and recommendations

Summary: findings and recommendations

Introduction

The pupils were chosen to participate in this project because they had a hearing loss or because they were hearing pupils with a deaf child in their class. The research focus, clearly, was related to deafness – for the pupils, however, being in school is not just about being deaf. Children commented on a whole range of aspects of school that they liked or disliked which might, or might not, have been related to their deafness. Similarly, hearing pupils did not necessarily focus on the deafness of the pupil in their class but would comment on other aspects which seemed particularly significant to them, such as the ability of the deaf pupil to help hearing friends with their maths homework. It is important not to lose sight of this 'bigger' picture, whilst acknowledging that all the pupils in the study identified a number of significant issues related specifically to deafness.

It is important to note too that no comment could be made regarding the pupils' access to the curriculum, their educational achievements or indeed how staff or other pupils saw individuals as fitting into the social life of the school. The research team can only comment on how the pupils themselves perceived these aspects of their school lives: it is not for us to say whether individual placements were appropriate or whether alternative settings would have been preferable. It was clear from the interviews that some pupils were very happy with their school situation; others accepted the type of schooling they experienced, but some felt isolated and excluded within a context that was supposed to include them. One or two pupils had such poor communication skills, both orally and in sign, that it was hard to see how they could be included in a mainstream context in any meaningful way. This identifies the importance of a range of provisions being available for deaf children and clearly challenges the notion that mainstream placement is right for all pupils.

The diversity of what deaf pupils say about their experiences is striking. This partly reflects the range of deafness and communication approaches being used within the sample of pupils interviewed. However, degree of deafness alone is not the most accurate predictor of how children perceive their situation. In presenting the data from the interviews, we have tried to reflect the mixed (and sometimes contradictory) comments made by pupils. This chapter draws out key themes and makes recommendations on the basis of what pupils say about their experiences of inclusion.

Deaf peers and deaf adults

Most of the deaf pupils see interaction with hearing peers as an advantage of mainstream provision but the majority also want deaf friends. The availability of other deaf pupils to communicate with is seen as important and is also identified and understood by hearing pupils involved in the project. Schools with groups of deaf pupils can provide this peer support and also raise the profile of deafness within a school. The presence of deaf pupils in a school enables staff to acquire and gain further relevant experience and expertise. For those deaf pupils placed individually in their local schools, key issues include how to establish links with other deaf pupils and how these links might be facilitated by the schools concerned.

Contact with deaf peers, older deaf pupils and a range of deaf adults helps deaf children develop a sense of personal identity. While deaf adults work in a range of teaching and other professional contexts in special schools for deaf children, they are involved in only some unit contexts and rarely in schools where pupils are individually included. It is important that both deaf and hearing pupils have contact with deaf adults, including deaf teachers. In the view of this research team, it is hard to think about inclusion being successful if we are thinking only about inclusive classrooms and not considering inclusive staff rooms.

Schools need to:

- **consider the role of deaf peers in the education of deaf pupils**
- **consider the role of deaf adults in the education of deaf pupils**

Teaching roles

Teachers of the deaf

Many deaf pupils involved in the project speak warmly about the teachers of the deaf in their schools, seeing them as being available to talk to and as being able to sort out problems. Clearly close and positive relationships are often formed, particularly in unit contexts where staff and pupils work together regularly. Pupils sometimes see these teachers as overprotective and 'nagging', which reflects an adolescent need to develop independence. Some pupils describe ways of circumventing agreed procedures, for example by appearing to be using appropriate equipment but failing to switch it on. In some contexts, unit or peripatetic teachers of the deaf clearly spend a great deal of time negotiating equipment and support needs with pupils. In other cases, pupils accept that support arrives in some lessons and not in others and are not sure of the rationale behind the level of support they receive.

Some pupils feel unable to discuss support issues, particularly problems with a member of the support staff, with the teacher of the deaf, in case this is then reported back to the member of staff concerned. It is difficult for young people in a school context to be critical of staff actions or procedures but this means that in some cases pupils appear to be receiving inappropriate support without this being identified. A mechanism for continuous consultation of all pupils about their educational needs is essential. It is interesting that during the interviews some pupils comment that the sorts of issues raised (such as what helps or hinders their achievement in school), have previously been discussed with their teachers of the deaf. On the other hand, some pupils feel that they have never talked about these things before and welcome the opportunity to do so.

Teachers of the deaf need to:

- **continue to support deaf pupils in relation to their academic, personal and social needs**

- **consult with pupils about their support**

Mainstream teachers

Pupils make many comments about mainstream teachers, as these are generally the teachers with whom they have most contact. As with all pupils, they like some teachers better than others but in the case of deaf pupils, this seems to be based on whether or not teachers use strategies in the classroom which allow the pupils to access the lessons. Strategies pupils find helpful have all been identified in previous studies (NDCS 1990, 2001a) and include:

- using demonstrations and practical activities

- allowing pupils to see the teacher's face clearly

- explaining key points

Unhelpful strategies include:

- talking a lot

- talking when facing the board

- not explaining tasks or homework clearly

Drawing attention to individual pupils' needs during lessons is seen as embarrassing. During the interviews some pupils got up and demonstrated particular teachers' teaching styles, including ' pacing up and down like a tiger'. While this generated a great deal of amusement in group interviews, where other pupils could immediately recognise teachers from the description of their teaching styles, it has serious implications: pupils state that they cannot follow what the teacher says due to the use of a particular teaching style or mannerism. Deaf pupils are entitled to expect teachers to modify their standard delivery to meet their needs: this is an essential step in providing inclusive education. Pupils generally report that teachers and teaching assistants who have had previous experience of working with deaf pupils use better strategies than those for whom this is new. Supply teachers are regarded as the least able to teach accessible lessons and often seem confused by the radio microphone, which, pupils say, they are likely to leave on the desk rather than use appropriately. Clearly, basic information for supply teachers in these contexts is essential.

If teachers are to be 'deaf aware' and to use appropriate teaching styles then this needs to be part of a whole school policy that is supported and monitored. Recognition needs to be given to the fact that teaching a class which includes a deaf pupil or pupils is a complex task, requiring a high level of knowledge and skill on the part of the teacher. This will include skills in appropriate delivery, the use of relevant language, effective use of visual support and collaboration with support staff. Ongoing, high quality continuing professional development is required if a real inclusive environment is to be developed. One short, after school INSET session is inadequate. If a school cannot provide its teachers with the knowledge, understanding and skills required to deliver lessons which are accessible to deaf pupils, then it erects a significant barrier to effective inclusion.

Teachers need to:

- **be aware of, and use, appropriate strategies during sessions without drawing attention to individuals**

Schools need to:

- **provide ongoing professional development for teachers**

- **monitor the use of appropriate classroom strategies**

- **provide a system for giving relevant information to supply teachers**

Equipment and noise

The use of audiological equipment is seen by pupils as an important element either facilitating or impeding inclusion. They find it difficult to follow lessons if teachers do not position radio microphones appropriately. They also find it uncomfortable if teachers shout when using a radio system, as a shout is amplified and often unexpected. Pupils speak with approval of teachers who are considerate enough to remove the microphone before shouting. It is clearly important that deaf pupils' audiological equipment is suitably adjusted so that sound is not inappropriately loud. Shouting may also indicate that a lesson is not well organised or controlled, a situation in which deaf pupils would find it hard to follow what was going on in any case.

A particular problem with using a radio system is that it is generally much more noticeable than hearing aids and this affects the pupils' image at a time when it is important to look like everyone else. This can be solved, to a certain extent, by the provision of behind-the-ear radio aids – an important issue for hearing-impaired services to consider. One key problem, however, is the need for the pupil to give the microphone to a teacher at the beginning of a lesson. Many pupils find this embarrassing and feel they are drawing attention to themselves. Sitting through a lesson without hearing often seemed the lesser of two evils. It is important for school staff to consider how to manage this. The teacher collecting the microphone unobtrusively from a pupil's desk may be an option, but the teacher needs to be alerted to the need to do this by a note in the register or a similar form of reminder.

Noise is consistently identified by pupils as a barrier to inclusion. At times this relates to inappropriate class management and at other times to poor acoustic environments. Pupils readily identify rooms or spaces that are particularly difficult to work in and it is important that teachers discuss these issues with pupils in order that steps can be taken to improve matters. One aspect of inclusion is creating an accessible learning environment; for deaf pupils, this may involve the use of sound field systems, acoustic ceiling tiles or fabrics to improving listening conditions. This would bring advantages to all pupils in a school, not only to those using hearing aids, cochlear implants or radio aids.

Teachers of the deaf need to:

- **ensure that audiological equipment is suitable for the context and is appropriately adjusted**

Mainstream teachers need to:

- **consider the effect of noise on hearing aid users**

- **identify ways of managing equipment unobtrusively**

Schools need to:

- **identify poor acoustic environments and seek to improve these**

Support

Adult support

Adult support to access the curriculum is found to be useful by many pupils. Some would like support for lessons where it is not provided. A number of pupils identify what they see as inappropriate support, which often involves adults intervening too early, not letting the pupil work things out for him/herself or giving too much help. 'Fussing' is a term used by some pupils in relation to some people giving support and this again links to the developing need for independence on the part of young people of this age. Some pupils acknowledge that it must be difficult for the support worker to sit and do nothing and believe this may be why adults intervene at the first opportunity. This points to the need for a high level of professional development for those undertaking this role, with an emphasis on how support for the teacher as well as the pupil can be undertaken. This might include making visual resources, modifying written materials, providing key vocabulary lists and working with identified groups for a particular task in addition to providing targeted support for the deaf pupils.

Hearing pupils note the tendency for deaf classmates to have a number of adults around them and wonder whether deaf pupils like this. The results of these interviews suggest that they do not. Deaf pupils particularly resent it when support staff are seen as interfering with relationships with their friends, by not allowing them to sit where they want, to chat or indeed just to be 'off-task'. It is difficult for support staff to ignore behaviour which may be seen as not helping pupils' academic development, particularly when they see this as their key responsibility. On the other hand, social inclusion may require the pupil to be involved in such episodes; it is difficult for support staff to strike the right balance and to know when and how to intervene. Providing support in a classroom context is a highly skilled activity and requires a high level of professional development. It also requires regular opportunities to meet and plan with mainstream teachers, teachers of the deaf and with pupils. Without adequate, timetabled opportunities for planning, support is likely to be less than effective in promoting inclusion.

Support staff need to:

- **continue to give effective, targeted support to pupils**

- **not over-support**

- **provide support for the lesson and the teacher as well as the pupil**

Schools and teachers of the deaf need to:

- **provide high quality training for all those providing support**

- **monitor support work**

- **provide timetabled sessions for support planning**

Peer support

Deaf pupils make more statements about friends than about any other topic. For most, this is a central part of school life. Learning to relate to other people is a key aspect of this stage of development and therefore any child who is not successfully included socially cannot be said to be included, even if s/he is succeeding academically. In most cases, social inclusion will support academic inclusion, as pupils work together and help each other with school work. As one pupil reports, it is friends that get her through school. On the other hand, other pupils' attitudes and actions can be a barrier to successful inclusion and some pupils report name-calling and bullying, though most appear to deal with this successfully and feel that teachers respond appropriately.

Relationships depend upon good communication and therefore for deaf pupils there are likely to be issues with this area. Many deaf pupils identify strategies they use to help them to interact with hearing peers, such as repeating utterances or writing things down. Some of the hearing pupils interviewed show excellent understanding of the communication needs of deaf people and identify strategies to use, such as looking at the person they are communicating with, repeating what they have said and choosing alternative words if the original proves hard to lipread. Hearing pupils also realise that it is much harder for the deaf pupil to communicate in a group than in a one-to-one situation and that they need to give support in these contexts. Some of the hearing pupils have learnt these strategies through experience, whilst others speak about sessions run by teachers of the deaf (often in Year 7), which involve deaf awareness and sometimes include drama and role play. Some of these are fairly high profile activities involving play productions in assemblies, thereby raising the awareness of everybody concerned.

The deaf pupils interviewed are ambivalent about hearing pupils being involved in deaf awareness activities. On the one hand, they do not like to be identified and embarrassed by having attention drawn to them individually, while on the other, they want people to use appropriate communication strategies with them and they do not want to answer repeated questions about deafness. Some pupils are happy to be involved in telling others about what it is like to be deaf but for others this is the last thing they want to do. Clearly deaf pupils need to be consulted about what they feel comfortable undertaking.

Deaf pupils themselves need the opportunity to discuss ways of communicating with hearing pupils, to identify how to deal with questions about deafness and how to express their needs. Making issues and strategies explicit can help pupils to feel more confident and can develop their skills in operating in an inclusive setting.

Working with hearing pupils on deaf awareness seems to be a particularly important element in promoting inclusion, considering the significant role of friends throughout school life. Ways of doing this need to be explored with colleagues within the school and also between schools, so that good ideas and resources can be shared. This is a whole school issue and part of the development of an ethos that recognises and values difference. Certainly in relation to many of the pupils interviewed for this project, it seems that the contexts where the pupils are most successfully included are those where deafness has a high profile. If difference is acknowledged and the school celebrates diversity within the school environment, the curriculum and the teaching approaches, then individuals can be more successfully included. Both deaf and hearing pupils talk about deaf pupils being seen as 'normal'. In an inclusive school the concept of 'normal' widens.

Schools and teachers of the deaf need to:
- **provide deaf awareness sessions for hearing pupils**
- **discuss the deaf awareness sessions with deaf pupils, being sensitive to individual concerns**
- **provide sessions for deaf pupils on inclusion strategies**
- **raise the profile of deafness within the school environment, the curriculum and teaching approaches**

Conclusion

Schools need to be continually developing their practices in relation to the needs of the pupils in their care. Deaf pupils have a wide range of complex needs that must be identified and provided for if these pupils are to be successfully included in a mainstream school. As this project demonstrates, both deaf and hearing pupils themselves are a key source of information regarding factors that facilitate or hinder inclusion.

All schools need to develop ways to involve pupils in their monitoring of the success of inclusive education. This research identifies practical ways in which pupils' perspectives might be embraced.

Glossary

BSL...British Sign Language, the language used by the Deaf Community in the UK.

Cochlear implant ....Electronic device with an external part containing a sound processor and an internal part surgically implanted in the ear to give a sensation of hearing.

Communication support worker...........In-class support worker for deaf pupils who use British Sign Language (BSL) or sign communication to support spoken English.

HIU..Hearing Impaired Unit, a facility with staff and resources designed to meet the needs of deaf pupils. It may or may not have an identified room or set of rooms and may be known by other titles, such as Resource Base.

Integration/inclusion ....These terms are often used interchangeably and in this report refer to the opportunity for all pupils to participate in a mainstream education context. The move from the use of 'integration' to 'inclusion' implies an onus on a school to adapt the learning/teaching context to meet individual needs and thereby become 'inclusive'.

Learning Support Assistant ....In-class support worker for deaf pupil.

Mainstream teacher ....A teacher who teaches mainstream classes of mainly hearing children.

Oral..The use of spoken language.

Peripatetic	A visiting teacher who supports teachers and pupils in a number of different schools. In the context of this report the teacher would be a qualified teacher of the deaf.
Radio aid	A person FM system that extends the range over which a speaker's voice is transmitted to the receiver worn by the pupil
Repertory grid	A knowledge elicitation technique. After identifying a small set of *elements* (e.g. objects, people) the participant is asked to define some *constructs* (attributes) which characterise those elements.
SEN	Special Educational Needs
Signing	The use of a form of signed language (may be British Sign Language, Sign Supported English or Total Communication).
Soundfield system	An FM system that amplifies a speaker's voice in a room.
SSE	Sign Supported English, the use of signs from BSL with fingerspelling used in English word order.
Teacher of the deaf	A teacher who has obtained an additional mandatory qualification as a teacher of the deaf.
Teaching assistant	In-class support worker (may also be known as Learning Support Assistant).
Total Communication	An approach to communication which may use British Sign Language, Sign Supported English, fingerspelling, and spoken and written English.

Unit...A facility with staff and resources designed to meet the needs of pupils with SEN (which may include deaf pupils). It may or may not have an identified base room.

Withdrawal ....Individuals or small groups of pupils being withdrawn from the main class lesson to undertake work with a teacher or teaching assistant.

Bibliography

British Deaf Association (1996) *The Right to be Equal* London: BDA

Corker M (1998) *Deaf and Disabled, or Deafness Disabled?* Buckingham: Open University Press

Davie R and Galloway D (1996) *Listening to Children in Education* London: David Fulton

Deaf ExMainstreamers Group (1996) *Mainstreaming Issues for Professionals Working with Deaf Children* Barnsley: DEX

Department for Education and Skills (2001) *Special Educational Needs: Code of Practice* London: DfES

Department of Health (1989) *The Children Act* London: HMSO

Greig A and Taylor J (1999) *Doing Research with Children* London: Sage

Gregory S, Bishop J and Sheldon L (1995) *Deaf Young People and Their Families* Cambridge: Cambridge University Press

Gregory S, Boulton A, Harris D, Lynas W, McCracken W, Powers S and Watson L (2001) *The Education of Deaf Pupils: Perspectives of Parents, Teachers and Deaf Adults.* A Supplement to *A Review of Good Practice in Deaf Education* London: RNID

Hill M, Laybourn A and Borland M (1996) *Engaging with primary-aged children about their emotions and well-being: methodological considerations* Children and Society 10: pp129-144

Hood S, Kelley P and Mayall B (1996) *Children as research subjects: a risky enterprise* Children and Society 10: pp117-128

Hornby G (1999) *Inclusion or delusion: can one size fit all?* Support for Learning 14: pp152-157

Iantaffi A, Jarvis J and Sinka I (2002) *Changing perspective: interviewing deaf pupils about inclusion* Paper given at the 6th Congress of the European Personal Construct Association, Florence, March 2002

Jarvis J, Sinka I and Iantaffi A (2002) *What do deaf children think about inclusion?* Paper given at the CEDAR conference, University of Warwick, March 2002

Lloyd J (1999) *Interaction between hearing-impaired children and their normally hearing peers* Deafness and Education International 1: pp 25-33

Lloyd-Smith M and Tarr J *Researching children's perspectives: a sociological perspective* in Lewis, A and Lindsay, G (ed) (2000) *Researching children's perspectives* Buckingham: Open University Press

Lynas W, Lewis S and Hopwood V (1997) *Supporting the education of deaf children in mainstream schools* 21: pp 41-45

National Deaf Children's Society (1990) *Deaf Young People's Views on Integration: A Survey Report* London: NDCS

National Deaf Children's Society (2001a) *My School in Scotland* Glasgow: NDCS

National Deaf Children's Society (2001b) *Deaf Friendly Schools: A Guide for Teachers and Governors* London: NDCS

Nunes T, Pretzlik U and Olson J (2001) *Deaf children's social relationships in mainstream schools* Deafness and Education International 3: pp 123-136

Powers S, Gregory S, Lynas W, McCracken W, Watson L, Boulton A and Harris D (1999) *A Review of Good Practice in Deaf Education* London: RNID

RNID (2001) *Education Guidelines Project – Effective Inclusion of Deaf Pupils into Mainstream Schools* London: RNID

Sheridan M (2002) *The Inner Lives of Deaf Children* Washington: Gallaudet Press

Sinka I, Iantaffi A and Jarvis J *Inclusion: what deaf pupils think* Paper given at the BERA conference, University of Exeter, September 2002

Stinson M and Antia S (1999) *Considerations in educating deaf and hard of hearing students in inclusive settings* Journal of Deaf Studies and Deaf Education 4: pp163-175

Stinson M and Lang H (1994) *Full inclusion; a path for integration or isolation?* American Annals of the deaf 139: pp156-158

Stinson M and Foster S (2000) *Socialisation of Deaf Children and Youths in School* in Spencer, P, Erting, C and Marschark, M (ed) *The Deaf Child in the Family and at School* Mahwah: Lawrence Erlbaum Associates

UNICEF (1989) *Universal Declaration of the Rights of the Child* New York: UNICEF

Wade B and Moore M (1993) *Experiencing Special Education: what young people with special educational needs can tell us* Buckingham: Open University Press

Notes

Notes

Notes